A LIFE CONSTRUCTED

Reflections on Breaking Barriers and
Building Opportunities

A LIFE CONSTRUCTED

Reflections on Breaking Barriers and Building Opportunities

DELON HAMPTON

WITH BOB KEEFE

PURDUE UNIVERSITY PRESS
WEST LAFAYETTE, INDIANA

Library of Congress Cataloging-in-Publication Data

Hampton, Delon.
  A life constructed : reflections on breaking barriers and
building opportunities / Delon Hampton with Bob Keefe.
    pages cm
  Includes index.
  ISBN 97w8-1-55753-658-7 (hardback : alkaline paper)
— ISBN 978-1-61249-317-6 (epdf) — ISBN 978-1-61249-
318-3 (epub) 1. Hampton, Delon. 2. African American en-
gineers—Biography. 3. Engineers—United States—
Biography. 4. Civil engineers—United States—Biography.
5. Delon Hampton & Associates. 6. Civil engineering—
United States—History. 7. African American business-
men—Biography. 8. Philanthropists—United States—
Biography. I. Keefe, Bob. II. Title.
  TA140.H296A3 2013
  624.092—dc23
  [B]
                                    2013023303

CONTENTS

FOREWORD

THE LIFE story of Dr. Delon Hampton, my friend and confidante, is truly inspirational and uplifting! In this book the reader will find a road map to success.

From his humble beginnings in Chicago, through the challenges of race and ethnicity in America, Dr. Hampton exemplifies the values of hard work and perseverance. He believes strongly that success is possible with self-determination, along with support from family, friends, and mentors.

I got to know Dr. Hampton in the late 1960s when he was a professor of engineering at Howard University in Washington, DC, while at the time I was beginning my career in government service and business in the nation's capital. We have remained close friends, and I was most impressed when he began his own engineering firm in the early 1970s. Again with grit, focus, determination, and a keen mind for business, Dr. Hampton created one of the most successful engineering firms in America. A leader in both national and international engineering associations and societies, Dr. Hampton has broken through many barriers in his field. And through forty years of directing his own firm, Dr. Hampton has built opportunities for numerous associates and employees, as well as the many others he has mentored.

A Life Constructed is a must-read for people of all generations. Dr. Delon Hampton's life is not only an African-American success story but truly an American success story!

Hon. Delano E. Lewis Sr.
Former US Ambassador to South Africa

Preface

THERE AREN'T too many big cities in America where I can't see one of the building blocks of the career and the life I have constructed as prime consultant or major sub-consultant.

You have probably seen them as well.

In Los Angeles, there are underground rail stations at Fifth and Hill Street, Civic Center, and Pershing Square and the double-barrel transit tunnel connecting them to Union Station. In Chicago, there are the new Comiskey Park, a section of that city's deep tunnel and reservoir system ("Deep Tunnel"), and the rail line connecting the city to Chicago O'Hare International. In Atlanta, there is the MARTA rail line that snakes its way through the hub of the South and the water treatment plants and the West Combined Sewer Overflow tunnel that keep the city humming. And in my company's home of Washington, DC, there is the Capitol Visitors Center through which every visitor to the US Capitol passes, the ever-bustling Gallery Place Chinatown complex and adjacent Verizon Center I pass each time I go to my office two blocks away, the Pepco headquarters building, Nationals' Baseball Stadium, the mixed use development, City Center, whose construction I am pleased to watch from my office window each work day, and Dulles International and Ronald Reagan Washington National airports I see each time I travel out of town.

Whenever I see these projects and others that my firm helped create in my more than fifty years as a professional engineer, they still make me feel proud.

But more than that, they make me feel very fortunate.

Today, the company I founded in 1973 has been involved with thousands of projects around the country. I have climbed to the pinnacle of my profession, and it has taken me all around the world. I have taught and mentored thousands of others, in the classroom and in my business and in my chosen field.

I am a very lucky man.

For a black kid who skirted gang violence and other hazards in inner-city Chicago; who was raised by an eighth-grade-educated mother who wasn't actually my mother; who overcame racial barriers during the time of Jim Crow and de jure segregation to earn a PhD, become a professor and then the CEO of a multi-million-dollar company I built from scratch with the help of others, I have much to feel lucky about.

And yet, the life I have constructed has come at a cost. It is still lacking some essential pillars that would have made it better, stronger, more satisfying.

An only-in-America story such as mine contains lessons for anyone seeking success. But it also holds the lessons of what the pursuit of such success can cost: friends and family members forgotten and lost, broken marriages, a childless life.

A few days before these words were written, I took a trip back to the very footings of the foundation of my life. It carried me back to a little town in Northeast Texas, where I met a cousin I knew better from business functions than from family gatherings. He was kind enough to take me for the very first time to the grave of the mother I never knew, as well as to those of the aunts and uncles and cousins I knew only in passing, and through the town in which I was born.

As I read the name on my birth mother's gravestone I was shocked that her given name, Alzadie, was spelled differently than the given name on my birth certificate, Elzatie. Which is correct? For now, I am assuming the spelling on the gravestone is correct.

My trip left me with an emptiness and a regret for never knowing my mother or many members of my family, but also with an appreciation for what my family accomplished and experienced, as well as a fullness for the successes I've been fortunate to experience.

Like the buildings, airports, train stations, and other structures that will be here long after I am gone, the life I have constructed was built from the ground up, with plenty of challenges and problems along the way. Its structure is complicated, yet simple. It is built solidly, but over the years has become a bit weathered and developed a few cracks.

This is my story.

Acknowledgments

First and foremost let me thank my wife, Sonia M. Hampton, for her support and encouragement during the writing of this book.

Two others who were with me all the way and made major contributions to the finished product are Dr. Janet Jones Hampton and Mrs. Gayle Jones Lewis. Their advice, counsel, hard work, and dedication to the completion of my book have proven indispensable. I could not have done it without their support.

In addition, the encouragement of my friends Elijah B. Rogers and Dr. Mary Conroy has been a source of strength.

My family, sisters-in-law Mrs. Meriel Douglas and Mrs. Mary K. Douglas, and my nieces, Dr. Leslie Douglas Churchwell, Dr. Susan M. Douglas, Mrs. Sarah Douglas Squiers, and Stacy L. Douglas, Esq., provided most of the family photographs contained herein. My cousin, Herman D. Douglas, provided text on Douglas family history, photographs, and a tour of our ancestral home. I am also grateful to the University of Illinois Archives for permission to reprint the picture of Dr. Ralph Beck (Faculty and Staff Press Release File, RS 39/1/11) and the Architect of the Capitol for the image of the US Capitol Visitor Center under construction.

Thanks a million also to all others who helped me on my journey through life. They are recognized herein.

Finally, I am especially grateful to Purdue University for honoring my family and me by publishing this book.

ONE

Points of Beginning

M Y EARLIEST memory is sitting on a footlocker in front of a window in the living room of our third floor apartment at 3853 South Langley Avenue on the South Side of Chicago, watching for Kat to come home from work.

Kat was the youngest of my two sisters, both of whom were teenagers when I was born. She and I were closer in years if nothing else, and her arrival home from work was a daily marker in my youngest years. Unfortunately, before I was old enough to know her better, Kat was gone. One of my last recollections of her was during her wedding, at a simple ceremony held in our family's apartment in Chicago with only a few family members present. She idolized her husband, Chat, and Kat and Chat were deeply in love. Tragically, their love affair ended shortly after their marriage, when

Kat died from tuberculosis. Chat subsequently slipped into alcoholism, which would ultimately help kill him shortly after the death of the wife he loved so much.

Vera was the older of the two sisters and left home when I was only about five years old. As a result I don't remember much about growing up with her either, though I also remember her wedding, which—in contrast to Kat's—was a huge affair at the Blackwell AME Zion Church. To this day it puzzles me how she and my parents could have afforded such a ceremony. Maybe it was because she was the first to get married. As the ring bearer at the wedding, I wore the fanciest outfit I had ever worn at the time: a black and white suit made from velvet, complete with a pair of short pants.

With Vera and Kat gone from our home, my world revolved around the woman I called my mother: Elizabeth Lewis Hampton. I never knew until I was much older just how hard life had been for her, but now that I do, I value and respect all she did for me even more.

The man I called my father, Uless Hampton, worked at the Tuthill Co., which literally helped build the city of Chicago beginning in the late 1800s when it started making bricks, and then later pumps, meters, and other equipment for the construction industry. I never had a serious conversation about anything with Uless, and never had much of a relationship with him either. The only thing I really learned from him was the desire and importance of reading and learning— and that came only after my mother had kicked him out of the house. When Uless departed, he left behind a small but significantly rich library of classics that I devoured, including books by Shakespeare, Churchill, and Plato. And when those books were done, I found myself becoming an avid visitor to our neighborhood library in search of more. How a man who worked in a pump factory and who never finished the eighth grade could become so attracted to such literature is both amazing and inspirational, and it fostered in me an interest in literature and arts that continues to this day. I saw Uless only twice after he and my mother divorced and he left our home: once after Vera convinced him he should give me some money I needed for school, and once when I was attending the University of Illinois and he came with other members of my family for a visit.

I recall meeting only three members of my father's family. Uncle Jack Hampton and his wife, Aunt Ann, lived in Kansas City, Missouri. I always looked forward to their visits, because they always brought me a gift. Uncle Charles Hampton operated a truck vending business from which he sold produce on Chicago's South Side. When I was a teenager I briefly worked for him. I remember that the work was hard and the pay was low.

While Uless was steeped in the classics, my mother was a simple woman. Her search for a better life had led her to the big city of Chicago with little more than her small-town Texas sensibilities and her unwavering faith in God. She worked at various times as an elevator operator and as a maid in downtown Chicago hotels. To make ends meet, she also cleaned houses, worked as a maid for wealthy Chicago families, and would occasionally rent out the spare rooms in our apartment.

Elizabeth Hampton's love life was just as tough as her work life. She was not very good at choosing mates. After Uless moved out, she became involved with a man who rented a room in our apartment. She and David Mixon eventually dated and got married, but his addition to our family was anything but blissful. Dave was an alcoholic who lost his job shortly after he married my mother. From that point on he lived solely off her meager earnings. He and I never got along and clashed frequently, coming close to exchanging blows on more than one occasion. I had no respect for him, and he had no respect for me. As a result, we coexisted in a state of armed neutrality, refereed by my mother.

Yet any love lost on Dave Mixon made the love between my mother and me even stronger. Despite being poor and black and living day-to-day on the South Side of Chicago, she somehow always found a way to make sure we had a good place to live, clothes to wear, and food on the table.

She could not afford health insurance, so the only medical attention I received before going to college (besides the standard preventative vaccinations in primary school) was one visit to a dentist. Instead, my mother would rely on homemade remedies she had learned in her country days in Texas to cure my many illnesses, ranging from jaundice to double pneumonia.

Once, when I had the croup, she took to the streets of inner-city Chicago to find a chicken—not just any chicken, but specifically a black chicken—that she killed and boiled. She rendered the bird's fat to make a foul-smelling salve that she rubbed on my chest and then covered me with a heated towel. She used the broth from the chicken as a soup to feed me. Later, when I was older and she recounted this story, she remained steadfast that this remedy had saved my young life, all but ignoring questions about how she ever found a black chicken on the streets of Chicago in the first place.

While the fat of a black chicken helped cure my lungs, it was peanuts that saved my eyesight, according to my mother. My eyes were always weak, and my eyesight a matter of great concern to my mother. To make my eyes stronger she began to feed me peanuts regularly. Miraculously, my vision began to improve. And I became addicted to the antidote my mother prescribed me: I still love peanuts to this day, especially when they're roasted in the shell.

Above all my mother relied on her excellent skills as a cook to keep me healthy. Our home was always filled with the rich aromas of home cooking and hearty spices, and there was always something good on the stove or on the table. Almost always it was country cooking that harkened back to her roots: fried chicken and collard greens, cornbread and chili, beef and macaroni and cheese, and all sorts of rich cakes and pies. Every once in a while I would go to bed hungry—not because my mother had not provided for me, but because I was a finicky eater and she never forced me to eat anything I didn't want to eat.

My favorite meal, without question, was Sunday breakfast. That's because that's when my Uncle Man (Burnette Lewis) and Aunt Alma, who lived a little further south in Chicago, would come over to have breakfast with us. Beaming above a plate of eggs, grits, and biscuits, Uncle Man would tell stories and jokes and talk to me in a way that neither Uless nor Dave Mixon nor any other man had talked to me in my life. Uncle Man was full of life and he was my favorite uncle. I always enjoyed his company.

My mother cooked not just for her family, but for others in our community, especially at her church. She was a devout Christian and a pillar in her congregation at the African Methodist Episcopal Church. If there were such a thing as a ministry of cooking and serving, Elizabeth Hampton Mixon was truly its finest minister. Without religion, my mother probably could not have survived all the hardships she experienced in her life. As a result she tried to give back however she could, whether it was with her cash or with her cooking.

My mother wanted me to come to know God, faith, and religion like she did. But I didn't. My impression of organized religion came from her preacher, whom I saw living high on the hog thanks to the hard-earned donations from my mother and others. He would often come to our house to beg for money for his personal use, while my mother struggled to put food on the table and clothes on my back. When I was about twelve years old and my mother decided I was old enough to make my own decisions about religion, I walked away from it. I would return a few times. During a stint in the US Army, for instance, I read the Bible from cover to cover and studied other religious books with other soldiers who were into religion. In graduate school I joined the local Methodist church, joined its youth group, and I even taught Sunday school. My roommate at the time, a devout Christian aptly named Henry Moses, who would become an inseparable friend, did his best to keep me on a faithful track. One of the many impressive things about Henry was his ability to reconcile religion and science. He would go on to earn a doctorate in biochemistry from Purdue and become a professor at Meharry Medical College. To this day his faith is still strong.

Despite the efforts of people I loved and respected, like my mother and Henry Moses, and despite my trying, I could not reconcile what I still see as the hypocrisy of many leaders and practitioners of organized religion. How could any religious person condone war, discrimination, greed, the rape of children, or other horrible offenses? And if there is a God, how could He let them get away with such behavior? I also simply cannot accept the concepts of God and the devil, heaven and hell, life after death. But even assuming there are such places, to me heaven sounds boring, and hell seems like not such a bad place. One might even be able to have a lot of fun in hell. Just think of all the great entertainers, comics, and thinkers who will probably be there.

Though my mother could not instill faith and devotion to religion in me, she did instill in me many other redeemable qualities, such as knowing right from wrong, fiscal responsibility, the value of hard work, and courtesy and respect for my elders. Back when I was growing up, before everyone had a car and while Chicago's "L" was still being built, the only reliable way to get to downtown Chicago was the streetcar. Whenever we went downtown, usually on shopping trips, which I grew to hate (I still detest shopping today), my mother made me give up my seat for any grown-up who was standing. Today when I ride public transit, I never see this happening. Instead, I notice that it is often the parent who gives up a seat to his or her child. To me that seems both unusual and unfortunate.

My mother also instilled in me a desire for a better life. She let me find the path to my future on my own, however. To the best of my recollection, we never had a conversation about my future. She was so busy trying to house and feed her family that she had neither time nor energy leftover to provide that sort of guidance to me. Likewise, she never helped me with my schoolwork either. Partly that's because she could only help so much, even if she could find the time to do so. My mother, due to circumstances beyond her control, never completed the eighth grade.

What my mother lacked in education, she made up for in her love for me. I would relish the chance to see her again and tell her how much I love her and appreciate all she did for me. But if I believed in an afterlife, I am sure she would be up in heaven, and I would likely be down in hell. Knowing my mother, though, I am sure she would never stop trying to convince St. Peter to let me join her.

*   *   *

For a woman who loved me like a son and whom I loved like a mother, my mother was not actually my mother at all.

I wasn't who I thought I was, either.

When I was growing up, Elizabeth Hampton spoke often of her place of birth, Jefferson, Texas, and of her relatives there. Some came to visit us in Chicago, and sometimes they stayed longer than a few days. My Uncle Valentine Lewis and his wife, Aunt Tot, for instance, moved in with us for a few years after work dried up in Texas. Uncle Valentine worked as a carpenter for a building contractor, while Aunt Tot worked as a clerk in a drugstore. From them and from my mother, I learned a little about the Lone Star State. To a boy from the streets of Chicago, Texas and everything about it seemed like a foreign land— a place where cotton and corn grew in endless fields, and cows and chickens roamed the prairies like the squirrels and pigeons in Grant Park. I envisioned cowboys and bands of roving Indians, and a sky that went on forever.

So when my mother decided one day when I was about ten years old that we needed to visit her home and meet the rest of my relatives, I naturally was ecstatic. It would be my first trip outside of Chicago. Riding on a real train was exciting enough; taking it to a place as mysterious and storied as Texas to meet members of my family for the first time only made it all the more titillating.

Little did I know just how revealing this trip would be for me.

It was around this same time that my mother told me something else: that my birth mother had died shortly after my birth in Jefferson, Texas, on August 23, 1933.

My birth mother, I was told, was named Alzadie Lewis Douglas. My father's name was Charles Douglas III. And my name at birth, I was told, was not Delon Hampton. It actually was Charles Douglas Jr.

Before her death at age twenty-five, I discovered, Alzadie had requested that my father give me to her sister and her husband to raise as their son. That sister was Elizabeth Hampton, and her husband was Uless.

Why my mother decided that I should be raised by her sister instead of my natural father and her family back in Jefferson, I do not know. I'm fairly sure, however, that my father didn't put up much of a protest to keep the baby whose birth coincided with the death of his bride.

Discovering my true past, of course, also prompted new questions when I was old enough to comprehend these things. I found myself wondering whether my injection into Elizabeth and Uless's family is what led to my all-but-nonexistent relationship with Uless, and if it led to their ultimate divorce. I wondered what my life would have been like if my mother had not made the decision to send me away from Texas. And I wondered if my birth father ever thought of me.

None of this entered my mind, however, as my mother and I walked into Chicago's Union Station bound for my first-ever journey to Jefferson, Texas. For a ten-year-old boy on his first trip out of town in the 1940s, the station seemed bigger than life itself. The limestone and marble corridors leading to our train seemed as long as city blocks. The massive barrel-vaulted skylight that ran the length of the Great Hall seemed like a window into the heavens. Shortly after my inaugural trip from the train station, those same skylights would be blacked out to make the building less of a target for enemy aircraft during World War II.

Our trip from Chicago took us out of the city, past the industrial communities of Joliet and Gary, Indiana, and into the plains of the Heart of Illinois, where corn and soybean farms filled the big windows of our train car. I remember the car being filled with people of all different types and colors, and being able to go wherever I wanted down the aisles of the train that led to the dining and other cars.

That changed when the train stopped in St. Louis. The conductor told us we had to move to a special car, near the front of the train where the noise was the loudest and the smoke from the engine was the worst. When we sat down in our new seats, I noticed that everyone in the car now looked like me and my mother. The car was filled with the smell of fried chicken, cornbread, and other home-cooked foods. Like my mother, most passengers in this car had packed their own food, because there was no longer any other choice if they wanted something to eat.

St. Louis, it seems, was at the edge of the Mason-Dixon Line. As a result, just like every other black person who traveled by rail in America between 1849 and 1954, when segregation in public transportation was finally ruled illegal, we were forced to move to a segregated car. As a boy growing up in urban Chicago, this was my first experience with segregation and racism, but it would certainly not be my last.

*   *   *

Jefferson, Texas, is a tiny speck of a town in the northeast corner of the state, near the borders of Louisiana, Arkansas, and Oklahoma. You wouldn't know it by visiting today, but there was a time when Jefferson was one of the biggest and most important gateways to the Southwest. Nestled along the Big Cypress River, it was once the busiest port in Texas—second only to mighty Galveston. The riverboats and barges that once filled the waters between Jefferson and the Port of New Orleans, like tractor-trailers that fill the interstate highways today, connected the American West to the rest of the country and the rest of the world.

In a state now dominated by the modern-day megalopolises of Dallas–Fort Worth and Houston, it's not surprising that little Jefferson tends to treasure its past. Almost every building and home in downtown Jefferson has a historical marker out front, from the Old Post Office to The Grove, a clapboard home built in 1861 that is now considered one of the most haunted houses in America.

One of the most haunting historical events that ever occurred in Jefferson, however, is less well celebrated. In 1868, with the wounds of the Civil War still deep and divisive, Jefferson erupted in racial violence that had to be quelled by army troops and martial law. Known as the Stockade Case, the incident began after George Webster Smith and four black men came to town in October of that year. Smith, a former Union officer and well-known Marion County resident, apparently got into an argument with a local former Confederate Colonel named R. P. Crump that led to gunfire. Smith and the black men were put in jail under the auspices that it was for their own protection. But on the night of October 4, 1868, a lynch mob of nearly a hundred hooded men who belonged to the Ku Klux Klan's Knights of the Rising Sun roared into town with torches and guns and took over the jail. According to accounts from the time, the Klansmen shot Smith through the bars of his jail cell window. They then dragged the black men to the nearby woods, lynching two of them while the other two escaped. After the US Army finally arrived in Jefferson to quell the violence, more than thirty suspected Klansmen were arrested and later put on trial before a military commission. Three of them were found guilty of murder; most of the rest went free.

My family owned a lot of contiguous land in Jefferson and in surrounding Marion County, Texas, and even to this day many of the streets and neighborhoods of Jefferson bear the name of my family—not Hampton, but Douglas. There is Douglas Street through the middle of town, Douglas Bottom out in the country, and the town of Douglas Chapel about ten miles to the east.

During my inaugural visit there in the 1940s, most of my time was spent with one member of the family or the other. When we weren't visiting, I was helping out on the farm or was out fishing, hunting, or otherwise spending time with my cousin Bubba and other relatives. Since we were out in the country and surrounded by family, we were not exposed to racism or segregation unless we went into town. I was, however, exposed to something else I had never seen in Chicago: homes without indoor plumbing. For the first time I used an outhouse, and I took baths in a big washtub filled with hand-pumped water instead of a shower connected to the city water supply.

All of this made for a great adventure for a kid from inner-city Chicago—so much so that a few years later I asked to go back to Texas during my summer vacation from school. It was another trip that would reveal more secrets of my past.

By then, I knew that I had been born Charles Douglas Jr. What I didn't know until that second trip to

Texas was that I was the second son of Alzadie Lewis Douglas and Charles Douglas Sr.

What I remember most about that first time I met Clarence was simply how elated I was to know that for the first time I had a brother. I was a teenaged boy who had been essentially raised by a single mother and two other females in our home in inner-city Chicago. Now, here I was in rural Texas again, surrounded by men who hunted, fished, and made their living off the land—including, I now realized, my own brother.

Throughout his life and from the moment I met him, my brother Clarence was a strong and vibrant individual. He was a hardworking leader who people gladly followed—including me. When I met him for the first time, he was already on his way to becoming a successful doctor. During the summer I met him, he was home from college and working in the men's locker room at a country club. I would go to work with him, helping him shine members' golf shoes.

At the time Clarence lived not in Jefferson but in Shreveport, Louisiana, about fifty miles away. One day he drove over to pick me up, not to go to the country club, but to go back to Shreveport. The reason: to meet the father I had never met before.

Charles Douglas Sr. was a baker who lived in Shreveport with his wife and with Clarence. During my second visit to Texas I would spend some time living with them too, although during the whole time my contact with my natural father was limited. I remember only one thing about that visit. One day my father took me to work with him. I had free reign of the bakery and all its operations, from the giant mixing machines and ovens to the wheeled racks and cases. What I remember most about that day was lunching on hot bread, fresh out of the oven, and drinking chocolate milk. During the weeks of my visit to Shreveport, I never had a conversation or interaction of any significant length or substance with my father. Except for the trip with him to his workplace, he ignored me.

Like me, Clarence did not get much from our father either. It was our uncle, Dr. Raymond D. Douglas (R. D.) and his wife Willie Mae (Aunt Bill), who were principally responsible for rearing and educating Clarence and leading him into the medical profession. R. D. Douglas was active in his community and in Texas state politics. He built, owned, and operated the local hospital in Jefferson, Texas. He also traveled extensively. To his credit, whenever he visited a city in which I resided, he would always call and take me out to dinner. He never gave me advice or counsel, however. I guess he decided taking care of one of his nephews was enough.

Clarence was R. D.'s hope and joy. He helped Clarence through college and medical school. He anticipated that Clarence would return to Jefferson, take over his medical practice, and run the hospital he had established. Clarence had other plans.

During his sophomore year at Meharry Medical College in Nashville, Tennessee, Clarence married his college sweetheart, Meriel LaBrame. Upon graduation he began an internship at Mercy Hospital in Cedar Rapids, Iowa. He did well at Mercy Hospital. So well, in fact, that he attracted the attention of a physician who convinced him to establish his practice in the nearby town of Belle Plaine, Iowa. Clarence decided it was a good idea and he and Meriel moved there, built a prosperous practice, and had two children. Clarence became an active and influential member of the community and for many years served as chairman of the Belle Plaine School Board. He also was the coroner for Benton County, Iowa.

Clarence and Meriel's marriage ended in divorce. Meriel took their children, Everett and Leslie, and moved to her hometown, Baton Rouge, Louisiana, where she raised them while teaching history as a professor on the faculty of Southern University. Leslie went on to become a very successful physician like her father, and she and her husband, Dr. Keith Churchwell, produced a talented daughter, Lauren. Everett never found himself. He died an untimely death after an asthma attack while attending a New Year's Eve party. Everett was very talented but appeared to me to have an unproductive life, I believe, because he was never able to cope with the breakup of his family.

Clarence subsequently married Mary Kearney, RN, a union that produced three very successful children: Susan, Sarah, and Stacy—a physician, a corporate executive, and a lawyer. Clarence was as strong and wise a father as he was a brother. My niece, Sarah Douglas Squiers, once told me of an incident that reflected her father's counsel. While she was in high school, a male student continually harassed her. She told her father and he advised her how to handle the matter. The next time it happened, she followed his instruction: She hit the bully on his head and then ran like hell. He chased her home but never harassed her again. Ironically, years later, from a prison cell, he wrote to her and asked for a date when he got out. Hope springs eternal.

Regrettably, my brother did not live long enough to read these words, dying of pancreatic cancer well before his time. When I saw Clarence the last time, just before he expired, he was a shell of the strong and strapping young man I had met during that second visit to Jefferson, Texas, and just a shadow of the stately and successful doctor from Iowa who in his later years would sometimes fly to Chicago in his own plane and spend time with me. At the time of his death, Clarence was totally helpless. He could not carry on a conversation for any significant length of time due to the pain medication he was taking. I am deeply saddened that his premature death prevented him from fully enjoying the success of his daughters and their children, but I know he can rest well. His children and grandchildren (Lauren, Miles, and Aiden) will make substantial contributions to society. He left a wonderful legacy.

Clarence was a much better brother to me than I was to him. From introducing me to our father, to his wise counsel, to his helping me secure a bank loan in my later years when my business was struggling to survive, he was always there for me. What saddens me the most about Clarence's passing is the realization that I did not enjoy his presence more during his life, and that his condition did not allow us the opportunity to say goodbye. The loss is mine.

There is one other thing I remember about visiting Jefferson, Texas, that sticks with me to this day. Like learning about Clarence, my father, and my roots, it forever changed and affected my life, although I wouldn't know it at the time.

Shortly after we arrived in Jefferson during my first trip there, my family gathered at the home of my Uncle Alvin Lewis. The adults were not there to socialize, however—they were there to work. As I stood with the other kids and watched from a safe distance on that hot summer day, the adults and a few of Uncle Alvin's friends took giant jacks, and to the awe of me and the other kids, they lifted his home right off of its very foundation. They then moved a long trailer underneath the home, lowered it carefully and slowly on to it, and moved the home to another location not too far away where they seated and anchored it onto its new foundation.

Why Uncle Alvin wanted to move his house, I cannot recall. I am sure he had his reasons, just as my mother, I am sure, had her reasons for deciding on her deathbed to uproot me from Jefferson, Texas, and send me to live with her sister in Chicago.

As a boy, the house moving spectacle left an impression on me in other ways. This was my first close experience with an engineering-related activity. And it very well may have been the initial step toward the engineering career that has defined my life.

Two

Footings and Foundations

MY ROOTS reach back to Texas. But the foundation of my life was built in the streets of Chicago's South Side.

Known as Bronzeville, the area of Chicago where I was raised got its name from the thousands of African-Americans from throughout the South and other parts of the country who moved there to escape racism and Jim Crow laws that followed the end of the Civil War, and after that, to find new opportunities in the midst of the Great Depression. In the early 1900s, during the peak of black America's northward migration, the community's population swelled to new highs, and it became known as both a magnet and a hub for African-Americans. Places like the Regal Theater attracted big-name black entertainers like Louis Armstrong, Lena Horne, Lou Rawls, Cab Calloway, and later the Supremes, the Temptations, and Gladys Knight & The Pips. The local Chicago Defender, the nation's foremost African-American newspaper, produced famous writers such as Pulitzer Prize-winning poet Gwendolyn Brooks. Andrew Rube Foster—another Texan who ended up in Bronzeville—created baseball's Negro National League.

Most of the people who lived there, however, were just like my mother: simple working-class folks looking for a better life, a better world, and a better place to raise their family. Connected by their common experiences and common dreams, these neighbors looked after each other. If an adult saw a child misbehaving, you could be sure that child's parents would find out about it and dole out an appropriate punishment—typically spanking and/or house confinement. Sometimes the neighbors would take care of the punishment themselves, usually with the full support of the child's parents. It was common for neighbors to share a meal or some groceries with one another, especially when times were tough. And while some people relied on charity and welfare, back in those days it wasn't something to be talked about; it was something to be hidden.

My friends were a great group of guys, and we did everything together. We formed neighborhood football, basketball, and baseball teams and challenged other neighborhood teams. Most of the time, we won. Every now and then, when we could scrape up enough money, we would walk down to Comiskey Park to watch the White Sox play baseball or the Chicago Cardinals play football, back before they moved to St. Louis and later on to Arizona. Decades later, my firm would be part of a team to help design and build the new Comiskey Park, right next to the old one where I spent my boyhood days.

When we weren't playing, or watching, sports. we were building things—dog houses, forts, soapbox cars, and scooters from scrap two-by-fours and old metal roller skates. The leader of our little group, Junior McDaniel, usually took the role of site supervisor. But I did my share of the engineering and construction of these boyhood projects, and I came to love taking whatever materials we could get our hands on and building whatever we could out of them.

Like the rest of my group, I was a latchkey kid. My mother worked outside the home and she couldn't afford a babysitter, so I had to learn early in life how to take care of myself. Usually the only one at home to meet me after school was our dog, Jack, who had followed my mother and me home one day and was a part of our life for sixteen years. I was responsible for feeding Jack and myself most days. I went to and from school myself, and—with my friends—often hopped on the streetcar for trips to museums, the aquarium, the planetarium, the Brookfield Zoo, and amusement parks. On weekends we might head down to the Savoy Ballroom or to local house parties to dance the night away. We were almost always on our own, with no adult supervision. In today's society such childhood freedom may seem almost inconceivable. But I can't help but think that the development of kids today has suffered because they don't have the freedom and the responsibility to explore and be creative like we did back then.

My boyhood was idyllic in some ways, but around us loomed the real world and all its problems. World War II was in full rage, and it touched everybody, even young boys growing up on the South Side of Chicago. Many days, we roamed the neighborhoods collecting metal—tin cans, scrap building supplies, whatever we could find—to raise money for the war effort. At home we saved money to buy ration stamps that my mother would use to buy sugar, butter, meat, and other staples that were in short supply. Through the newspaper and the radio, we followed the horrific events unfolding in unimaginably faraway places like Normandy, Salerno, and Iwo Jima. We saved our pennies to buy Defense

Stamps at school, and our parents saved to buy Defense Bonds.

The real threats to me and my friends, however, were much closer to home. While my immediate neighbors were congenial and caring with each other, we didn't have to wander far before things got rough.

Across the street from where we lived was the Ida B. Wells Homes project, which would become the stereotype for the problems with public housing before it was demolished in 2011. When I was growing up in the 1940s, the project had yet to earn its infamous reputation as a haven for gangs and drug dealers—but it and other surrounding developments were well on their way.

My friends eventually could be defined by the two groups they hung out with: the "squares" and the "junkies." Some of my friends became involved in drugs and ended up joining the junkies, but my closest friends and I were content being squares. Usually there wasn't any tension between the two groups; that's just the way our world worked. Except for some friendly competition on the basketball court or on the football field, the squares and the junkies coexisted most of the time with no problems and no indifference to each other.

That wasn't always the case, however. The older I got, the rougher it got. One night, my friends and I were hanging out in front of the corner store in our neighborhood, just down from the old streetcar barn. We were minding our own business, talking about girls or sports or whatever was the most important topic of the day. Across the street we saw a group of guys we knew were in a gang. They started walking toward us. We didn't think anything of it—as mentioned, that's the way our world worked. Then we heard shots ring out. When we realized it was us they were shooting at, we ran like hell. They started chasing, and at that point it was every guy for himself, and God help us all. As I ran, I heard more shooting behind me. I have no idea if they were firing at me or at somebody else or just shooting into the air. I was too scared and too focused on getting away to turn back for a look.

On another night, on another street corner, another friend of mine with whom I used to play football and basketball wasn't as lucky. He too was standing there minding his own business when the shooting started. He went down, hit by a bullet right in the face. He lost an eye forever.

By the time I was in grammar school our neighborhood was surrounded by gangs. Avoiding them became a way of life. We traveled in groups and we took care of our own whenever we went to school or anyplace else. When we didn't have anybody to watch our back, we had to sneak through the back alleys with hopes that we wouldn't encounter any gangs. Even when you had somebody else with you, it could be unsafe. One night, my friend Delaney and I were hanging out when a group of boys from another neighborhood came across us. They started calling us names and pushing us around. Then the fists started flying. Delaney and I fought back, and we got away. But as we nursed our bruises, bumps, and cuts in the silence after the fight, we both knew our lives and our neighborhood were changing.

My mother was usually oblivious to anything that happened after I left home and shut the door behind me. But she also had an uncanny knack for keeping me safe. Each time my friends got into serious trouble or got hurt, she kept me out of harm's way by keeping me home. "Toots," she would say, using her pet name for me, "you've been runnin' too much. Stay home tonight." Though my mother didn't know about what happened outside of our home, and though she gave me the freedom to do whatever I wanted most of the time, I am sure it was my fear of hurting her—and facing her wrath—that kept me out of gangs and set me on the path I would take in life. My mother was a wonderful woman who loved to laugh and joke and have a good time. But when it came to raising me and keeping me on the straight and narrow, she did not play.

Despite being raised by two people who never got to high school, school to me was easy and enjoyable—so easy, in fact that I often found myself pulled into the principal's office for talking and misbehaving in class. Occasionally my mother had to come to a meeting with my teachers and/or my principal. My most dreaded task was to have to go home and tell my mother she had to take a day off from work to attend a meeting at school. We were always strapped for cash and this meant she had to lose a day's pay. Depending on what I did, it could also mean a whipping. My father, Uless Hampton, whipped me only once. My mother observed this whipping and felt it was too severe. Consequently, she forbade him to whip me ever again and assumed that responsibility herself. She was very good at it.

Fortunately for me, the assistant principal at Oakland Elementary School, Mrs. Jackson, saw something good in me and protected me at critical times. They say it only takes one teacher to change a child's future. For me, it was Mrs. Jackson. Once I was hauled into principal's office for bad behavior and was to be sent to one of the city of Chicago's schools for incorrigible boys. Mrs. Jackson saved me from that fate. If I had been sent to Mosley Elementary School, my future might have been very different. Instead, I finished Oakland Elementary at the age of twelve. The principal decided that our class had caused too many disciplinary problems during our tenure so he would not allow us to have a graduation ceremony. They handed us our diplomas and sent us home. The next school day (I graduated mid-year) I headed for Wendell Phillips High School.

I was at Wendell Phillips for all of one academic year, during which I concluded without a doubt that I was wasting my time there. I wasn't learning anything, and as a result I had no good reason to go. By the end of my first semester I had cut class more than thirty times. Even so, I passed everything, and my mother, to the best of my knowledge, was never informed of my cuts. Furthermore, my absences had not precipitated any action or comments from teachers, nor administrators.

By then, I had begun to set some goals for my life. I had watched how tough of a time my mother had, and I wanted to have a better life and the opportunity to help her. Even though I hardly knew anybody who had gone to college, I knew that I had to go. I defined my goals even further than that. I decided that I wanted to finish high school by the age of sixteen, to finish college by the age of twenty, to get a PhD by the age of twenty-two, and earn $10,000 a year. Since I prepared my mother's income tax returns, I knew she never grossed as much as $6,000 a year, thus a year's earnings of $10,000 represented a lot of money.

To do this, though, I knew the first thing I had to do was to get out of Wendell Phillips High School. I found a way to do that with the help of my uncle and aunt. Uncle Man and Aunt Alma had recently moved further south in Chicago. I decided that going to high school in their school district offered a much better path to a good education and to fulfilling my personal goals. Therefore, during my second semester at Wendell Phillips, I finagled my way into a transfer to Englewood High School using my aunt and uncle's address.

It took me more than an hour and two streetcars each way to get to and from Englewood High School. It was a long way, especially on days when it snowed. Yet moving to Englewood was a major milestone in my life, and one of the keys to my future success. I made friends quickly there, and by the start of my sophomore year, I was a member of the student body. I was on the school's track team (I ran the hurdles, low and high, and sprints, and participated in the shot put and long jump). I swam the breaststroke on the swim team. And I played football.

Our football team was lousy, but we had fun. It was lousy not because we had poor players but, principally, because we had a lousy coach. He taught us nothing of value while, at the same time, making extra money by pretending to be our coach. We generally won only one game a season—against Hyde Park High School. Nevertheless, our team bonded, we played the best we could, and we enjoyed our time together.

My teammates became some of my best friends. Ray Harden and Ed Fleming were two of the closest, and we were inseparable. Ray's parents had invested in real estate and were well off. Even in high school, Ray had a car and we got around quite a bit. Ed and I were the poor guys but Ray never flaunted his financial advantage. My other close friends included Earl "Turk" Doty and Donald "Doc" Greenlee.

Uncle Man and Aunt Alma's sons, Raymond and Junior (Burnette Lewis Jr.), also went to Englewood, but we were never very close so we had little contact during our high school careers. We developed different sets of friends and values and consequently operated in different social circles.

I did not do much dating in high school. I lacked the confidence that I was attractive to girls. I was not a good conversationalist, and I did not dress well. Nevertheless, my heart belonged to Tina Hill. She was petite, beautiful, and everything I thought I wanted in a woman. I was too much in awe of her, however, to ever make any advances. I was kind of her lap dog. I became friends with her family but I do not recall ever asking for a date, although she often invited me to her home. As a result, her sisters, Shirley and Sylvia, and I became and are still very good friends. Even to this day I periodically visit them and their families in San Diego. Those visits are a lot of fun. Tina has become a recluse, but her sisters and their families are as lively and as vivacious as ever.

The day I graduated from Englewood remains vividly etched in my memory. Our principal loved music and theater, and personally directed the production of all graduations. As a result, Englewood graduations seemed like Broadway productions. I still get a thrill when I hear in my mind's ear the voices of our sopranos singing during our graduation performance. And I still remember too—although a little more hazily—jumping into Ray's car and heading for the parties after the ceremony. I didn't eat dinner that night, and before long the alcohol overwhelmed me. When Ray and Ed dropped me off at the end of the evening and my hat blew off, I could only laugh as I watched it roll down the street with Ray and Ed in chase.

Years later I would find myself beside Ed Fleming in hospice as he lay dying. Sitting next to my friend in the last days of his life as he struggled with prostate cancer was a heart-wrenching experience. But I am glad I was able to be with him. Unfortunately I did not get a chance to say goodbye to Ray, who also died of cancer. I learned of his death when I was planning a trip to Dallas and sought to invite him and his wife, Evelyn, to dinner. I had not seen them in a very long time. When I called to set up the dinner, Evelyn, in her gracious and apologetic way, told me she would be happy to have dinner with me but Ray had died two months earlier. I was shocked.

Switching to Englewood High School was the most important decision of my young life. If I had not made that decision I probably would still be hanging out on street corners in my old neighborhood, or worse. I probably never would have gone to college or entered the profession of civil engineering.

THREE

Life Construction

D URING THE summers before I graduated from Englewood, I made it a point to go to the career fairs held at the Illinois Institute of Technology, not far from my home. To this day, IIT holds these highly successful career fairs, where a suit and tie is required for entry and where thousands of Chicago-area young people find jobs, or at least a path to the job they want. In September 2012, as the country was still recovering from the worst recession in recent history, according to a local television station the IIT career fair attracted so many employers and other exhibitors that some had to be turned away.

Back when I was a high school student visiting the IIT career fairs, I didn't know exactly what I wanted to do for a living. But I had some general ideas. The three areas of most interest to me at the career fairs were civil engineering, architecture, and chemistry. I liked civil engineering and architecture because I like to build things. I liked chemistry because it was an area of interest of my sister Vera.

To pursue a career in these fields, I knew I had to go to college. That was already a given, however. I always knew I wanted to attend college. I knew this despite the fact that during my formative years I had no advice on school or careers or education from any adult. Since my mother had only an eighth grade education, it was impossible for her to give me guidance on issues like these, although she supported me 100 percent once I made a decision, even though she may not have fully understood the implications of that decision.

When it came time for me to apply for college, I chose the University of Illinois. I requested placement in the area of architecture and was accepted. Shortly after I applied, however, I began to realize that architecture required artistic skills, and I just didn't feel like I had the artistic skills that I needed. I changed my admissions request and asked instead to be admitted to the College of Engineering—specifically, the Department of Civil Engineering. Facing my artistic limitations came at a critical moment. This was probably the most important decision of my life at that time.

In January 1950, at sixteen years of age, I packed my mother's wardrobe trunk and a suitcase and, with a kiss, boarded a train headed for Champaign-Urbana, home of the flagship campus of the University of Illinois system. To the best of my knowledge I was the first person in the Hampton family to go to college.

With me on campus were my old high school football teammates and friends Turk Doty and Doc Greenlee. Following Doc's lead, I had arranged to pledge and move into the Kappa Alpha Psi fraternity house at 707 S. Third Street. I was not apprehensive about this move because I knew Doc Greenlee would look out for me. I spent an enjoyable four and a half years at the Kappa house. I waited tables and washed dishes in fraternity houses for meals and waited tables at country clubs for cash. I was helped significantly by the counsel provided by some of the returning military veterans, who scared me nearly to death about the possibility that I might flunk out. I took their advice and admonitions to heart, and I stayed in school.

Unlike Chicago, the cities of Champaign and Urbana back then were more like small towns in the South than small cities in the Midwest. It didn't take long before I realized that the Jim Crow practices I had first experienced as a boy headed to Texas were also present there. If a black man or woman tried to move off campus, Jim Crow would rear its nasty head and keep that person from moving into an all-white neighborhood. Other racist practices were more subtle but ever-present even on campus as well. Once, our fraternity team was playing in a key intramural volleyball game. A white referee called what was clearly a bogus foul against us at a crucial point in the game, and we lost. The white team we lost to went on to win the intramural championship. Another instance involved Thomas Floyd, a black fraternity brother of mine who was a high jumper as well as the captain of the university's track team. During one season the team was invited to participate in a track meet in the South—but with a caveat: The university was told it could not bring along any of its black members. The university agreed, causing a furor on campus. The black members of the team graciously bowed out, however, and the team traveled south to compete without them. During that time it was common to prohibit schools from non-segregated states to bring black team members to compete in sporting events in the South. Even religious institutions participated in this and related types of discrimination. Such memories are another reason I find it difficult to support organized religion.

Despite all of this, some of my best memories are of my time at the University of Illinois. When not in class, we competed in intramural choir competitions, as well as intramural sports such as football, baseball, and volleyball. Through these activities I made a lot of good friends—friends I have to this day. My group of fraternity brothers was very close and some of my dearest friends came from my time at the Kappa house. Many of us still meet each New Year's Day, in Chicago, to remember the good times, to honor those who have left us, and to celebrate our friendships.

My Kappa Alpha Psi connection led to my election to the Panhellenic Council and my appointment to serve on its board. This came with an additional perk: I also served on the selection committee for homecoming queen. Admittedly, I did not do a good job. Quite simply, all the young ladies looked so good to me that I could not find clear distinctions. They all got high marks in my book. In a subsequent election, though, a black female student, Clarice Davis, was elected homecoming queen. All the black students walked around with their chests puffed out in honor of her win. She beat Jim Crow—and by extension, so did all the rest of us.

I also picked up a new diversion while at the University of Illinois that I love to this day. One day during my free time at the university's Union Building, I learned to play bridge. I was instantly hooked on the card game. There were always revolving bridge games in the Union Building and rather than go back to my room and study, I would often play bridge. As a result, my sophomore year grades suffered but I learned my lesson. I had to exercise more discretion and make wiser choices, and I did. But to this day I still enjoy a good game of bridge.

The College of Engineering subjected me to a wide range of courses. One of the required courses in my curriculum was Soils and Bituminous Materials. The course may have seemed as boring as, well, dirt to some. But to me it was incredibly stimulating. Subsequently, I took two courses from a very dynamic professor—Dr. Ralph B. Peck, one of the greatest geotechnical engineers in history—and my future was sealed. It didn't take long before Ralph became my mentor and friend for life. He never refused a request for assistance from me and, through his support and stature, he helped significantly to advance my career. More than anything, he sealed my future in engineering. Before he passed away I twice tried to get Ralph a major award from the National Academy of Engineering (NAE), our nation's most eminent honorific engineering society. Unfortunately I failed. I feel the only reason for my lack of success is that civil engineers and their contributions to society are not valued as highly by the NAE membership as those of other engineering disciplines. Therefore, even though during his life Dr. Peck was recognized worldwide as one of the top four greatest geotechnical engineers, it was not enough for his fellow members of the NAE to honor him. That's sad, and one of the reasons I will not make a legacy gift to the NAE.

There was something else that would influence my career path, and convince me to alter my focus from construction engineering to geotechnical engineering. Once again, racial discrimination played a role.

During the spring semester of my sophomore year I began a search for employment for the upcoming summer. My goal at that time was to be a construction engineer so I interviewed with construction firms and the Illinois Department of Transportation. Even though this was during the height of the design and construction of our country's Interstate Highway System, I could not get a job offer from a private sector firm, while my fellow civil engineering students were receiving multiple offers. My only offer of summer employment was from the Illinois Department of Transportation (IDOT). However, I was not allowed to become a construction engineer or inspector, which is what I wanted to do. Instead, I spent the two summers prior to my graduation from the University of Illinois designing traffic light installations for intersections in suburban Chicago.

During those two summers when I worked at the IDOT District 10 office in Chicago, I saw only one other black person working as an engineer. He was a permanent engineer employee working not as an engineer, but as a draftsperson. Later in my career I came across a total of two black engineers who served as district engineers for state highway departments. I carry nothing but admiration for those men because of the discrimination and hardships they must have suffered to achieve the success they attained in their careers.

By the time I reached my senior year at the University of Illinois, I still wanted to become a construction engineer. Therefore, when I started looking for a job—this time, a permanent job—all of my interviews were with such firms. As hard as I tried, however, I got no offers. One man, representing a construction firm, gave me a clue as to why. He told me his firm had one Negro engineer and did not want any more. He did not offer a reason.

One thing I knew I did not want to do was return to designing traffic signal installations for the Illinois Department of Transportation. Fortunately, one of my fraternity brothers who had graduated the previous year from the College of Engineering's graduate program wrote me and inquired if I would be interested in a position as an instructor in the Department of

Civil Engineering at Prairie View A & M College in Texas. I accepted. There was only one problem: Early in the semester in which I was scheduled to graduate, I learned I would be one semester hour short of the requirement to receive my bachelor's degree in Civil Engineering. No degree meant no job at Prairie View. So the summer following my senior year I had to take a one-hour course to make up the difference. I turned to my mentor and friend Dr. Peck. He helped me by allowing me to take a one credit hour special project course in his soil mechanics laboratory. This choice helped to set the stage for the rest of my life. In addition to earning me the one semester hour I needed to graduate, being associated with and learning from Dr. Peck and his faculty convinced me that I wanted to spend the rest of my life not in construction engineering but in the area of geotechnical engineering.

It was with this realization in mind that I left the University of Illinois and boarded a train to Chicago after finally completing my graduation requirements in 1954. I was buoyant and eager to face the challenges ahead, but it also was good to get back to Chicago and be with my family and closest friends for a few weeks before beginning my job as an instructor at Prairie View A & M College. While I was away, my mother had moved from Thirty-Ninth and South Langley to

Sixty-Third and South Ingleside, where she was managing a small kitchenette apartment building for a family she once worked for as a maid. The rent was free for the apartment she occupied. She collected rent payments for the owner and received a portion of the money collected as compensation for her work as manager. Her earnings were not that much but were enough to let her live comfortably, when coupled with the money that I later would give her each month once I began my engineering career.

I arrived by train at Prairie View A & M College and checked into the faculty dormitory to begin my teaching career. When I arrived I found I had a roommate, Professor Carl Weems, and we began to bond. When I met with Dean C. L. Wilson, I learned that I would be teaching engineering mechanics and materials courses. Dean Wilson was a fine man who cared deeply about his students, the School of Engineering, and Prairie View A & M College. He also let me do my job. I was a tough grader and demanded a lot from my students because I knew that to survive in the engineering world they had to be tough and well prepared. Some complained to Dean Wilson about my grading, but to his credit he never asked me to lighten up. Like me, most of the rest of the engineering faculty were young and energetic, and I believe we gave students the skills and opportunity to become excellent engineers.

Along with my roommate Carl Weems, I became close to Pearl and Eddie Martin at Prairie View A & M. Eddie Martin was a professor of biology and later became head of the Biology Department. Pearl was a professor in the College of Arts and Sciences. She also was a professional artist—and a gifted one at that. She was kind enough to give me one of her paintings, which to this day hangs on my office wall.

In 1955, during the middle of my first semester at Prairie View A & M, I got a greeting from Uncle Sam. He wanted me to serve my country in the US Army. I was drafted. When I went in to tell this to Dean Wilson, he indicated that he could request an exemption on my behalf due to my position at the university. I said thanks but no thanks. Truth be known, I could not see myself remaining at Prairie View for an extended period of time. I knew I wanted to return to graduate school to pursue a master's degree in geotechnical engineering; the army gave me a reason to leave.

At the end of the fall semester I turned in my grades, said goodbye to my co-workers and friends, and returned to Chicago. On the appropriate date I reported for duty and, shortly thereafter, was on my way to Camp Chaffee, Arkansas, for basic training. I did not recognize it at the time, but I was inducted into the army just a few weeks before the termination of the original GI Bill. It was another stroke of luck that changed my life. As a result, I received federal financial support for my graduate school education.

I spent eight weeks in basic training at Camp Chaffee in northwest Arkansas. For a while I was the recruit platoon leader, but I was not enough of a good ol' boy to keep the position for my entire tenure. For a time I considered applying for officer candidate school, but I decided against it when I learned that there were no slots open in the US Army Corps of Engineers.

At the end of basic training I was sent to Fort Belvoir, Virginia, to become a water purification specialist. The best part of my tenure there was Fort Belvoir's close proximity to Washington, DC, where I spent most of my spare time. My Prairie View A & M friend, Professor Pearl Martin, had provided me with an introduction to a young lady attending Howard University, whom I dated. This made my stay even more enjoyable. In addition, while in Washington I was allowed to stay at the Kappa Alpha Psi fraternity house rent-free, which was great aid to a poor soldier. I enjoyed my time at Fort Belvoir, but before I knew it, I had completed my training and was transferred to Fort Bragg, North Carolina, and was assigned to the Twentieth Engineer Brigade.

My fellow soldiers of the Twentieth Engineer Brigade were a fine group of men. Most were engineers, and practically all were college graduates. We had a lot of fun on base together—going to the movie house, reading books, and just sitting around in bull sessions. Unfortunately, due to segregation in the South, our fun and socialization ended at the borders of the base. We were not able to socialize off base.

I came across some old friends at Fort Bragg too. One of my fraternity brothers from the University of Illinois, for instance, was a US Air Force officer and pilot stationed there. We socialized together and once caught a ride on an Air Force plane to Indianapolis. Upon arrival, we hitchhiked from Indianapolis to Chicago and had a wonderful long weekend.

It was during my time at Fort Bragg that I got word that the man I knew as my father, Uless Hampton, had died. I returned to Chicago for the funeral. While we were never close, he was the man I considered my father. As a result, on my next trip to Washington I contacted one of my old fraternity brothers, who was an attorney, with a request.

I asked him to process the paperwork to officially change my name from Charles Douglas Jr. to Delon Hampton.

Four

Building the Next Level

O NCE I realized my future wasn't in the army, I began thinking about where to pursue my master's degree. My experience at the University of Illinois convinced me I wanted to be a geotechnical engineer. Since it was then generally thought that one should not get all of his or her degrees from the same institution, I decided to apply for admission to Purdue University, a school with an outstanding reputation in geotechnical engineering. Purdue had an additional attraction for me: It was relatively close to my Chicago home.

I applied to Purdue University's graduate school for admission to its master's degree program in civil engineering, and was accepted. So in January 1957, upon my discharge from the army and after a brief stopover back in Chicago to see my mother and friends, I headed for West Lafayette, Indiana, home of Purdue.

Indiana at that time was not a hospitable place for people of color. Today, African-Americans make up less than 3 percent of the population of West Lafayette; back in the 1950s when I arrived, there were even fewer of us—at least that's what it felt like to me. As a result, I could not find any place that would rent me a room in West Lafayette. Instead, I had to rent a room in the home of a black family several miles from campus in Lafayette.

Even so, it wasn't long after I arrived at Purdue that I realized that the gods had smiled on me once again. It didn't seem that way at first. I had wanted a research assistantship in my primary department of interest, geotechnical engineering, but it turned out there were no assistantships available. Instead, I was assigned a half-time research assistantship under Professor Eldon Yoder that commenced with my first semester of graduate study. Working for Professor Yoder allowed me to study and work in that area even though I was not a part of the Geotechnical Engineering Department. Just as important, Eldy became my mentor and a very good and dear personal friend. Under his guidance, I developed my thesis topic, "Stress-Strain Properties in Cohesive Soils Under Dynamic Load," and this became my first published paper.

Toward the end of my work on my master's thesis, Professor Yoder asked if I would like to study for a doctorate. This was not in my original plans. I wanted to go into the private sector after my master's degree studies were completed. But once again, as the end of this segment of my education approached, I received no private sector job offers, even though other graduate students did. As a result, I accepted Professor Yoder's offer to pursue a doctorate, and, as he directed, I made an appointment with Professor K. B. Woods, the chair of the School of Civil Engineering, to get his blessing for doctoral study. He said yes so I went back to Professor Yoder to tell him the good news and to find out what I would be working on. Unfortunately there were no funds available to allow me to continue my research in soil dynamics. Of the projects he had available with adequate funding, I chose the topic "Variability of the Engineering Properties of Brookston and Crosby Soils." This study took three years to complete, and I received my PhD degree in June 1961. Concurrently, another professor, Dr. Gerald A. Leonards, offered me a half-time teaching assistantship in his area of soil mechanics and foundation engineering, which I accepted. That, along with my half-time research assistantship and the GI Bill, meant I was financially secure for the remainder of my stay at Purdue

University. I am greatly indebted to Professors Yoder and Leonards, who at critical times in my academic career at Purdue provided me with such good counsel and support. In addition, I greatly appreciate the friendships I made while at Purdue, which helped me have a vibrant and happy life despite a relatively inhospitable social environment.

Partly what made my time at Purdue more comfortable was religion, oddly enough given my previous eschewing of church and organized religion. When I arrived in West Lafayette I decided to become active in the Methodist Church. I taught a Sunday school class of preschool girls and even joined the Methodist Youth Group. It was there that I met two ladies, Jo Jones and Thelma Battershell, who became very good friends and made my stay much more enjoyable. I greatly appreciate their friendship. Through the church I also met a couple from West Lafayette who agreed to rent me a room in their home. This put me much closer to my laboratory, where I spent a lot of time, and made my life a lot easier. I also kept up my bridge playing while at Purdue, and my very special friend and fellow graduate student, Dr. Milton Harr, taught me to appreciate classical music, fine art, and fine wine—all of which I continue to enjoy to this day. Milt encouraged me to study the Russian language and also talked me into translating an important Russian geotechnical engineering textbook into English. This I did, and we made the translation available at no cost to others.

I earned my master's degree in civil engineering from Purdue in 1958. Three years later, in 1961, I earned my PhD, also in civil engineering, from Purdue. What made my graduation ceremonies all the more special was that they both occurred in the presence of members of both the Hampton and the Douglas families. My mother, sister, and brother and his family all attended both of my Purdue graduations—something I greatly appreciate. I also am appreciative of Purdue University for giving me my first national honor in 1982, and an honorary doctorate in 1994. The College of Engineering also gave me the opportunity to give an invited lecture on the future of transportation at a national symposium it sponsored related to the future of engineering.

I finished my engineering education at Purdue, but my graduation was just the beginning of my worldly education. I decided to spend a summer in Europe. I had saved some money during my graduate studies at Purdue, and with that cash—along with the helpful hints in Arthur Frommer's book *Europe on $5 a Day*— I managed to have a great and enlightening time in the Old Country.

My trip started with a flight to Madrid, where I enjoyed the treasures of the city, including my first bullfight. It was a bittersweet experience because it was obvious that the bulls could not win. In addition, along with a young Scandinavian man and a young American woman, both of whom I met at the local youth hostel, I toured Madrid. The Scandinavian and I also toured the home of the famous Spanish painter El Greco and enjoyed his art and his city. From there I went to Vienna, Austria, where I enjoyed an opera performance and—during the intermission—the best glass of port wine I've ever tasted.

My next stop was Florence, Italy, where I viewed the works of great art masters. Then it was on to Venice, where I was fortunate to stay at a youth hostel where the students adopted me and showed me a great time. I even was allowed to purchase my meals at student prices, which helped me live within my $5-a-day budget. From Venice I traveled to Rome, where I took the opportunity to participate in a public audience that the Pope had while I happened to be standing in St. Peter's Square. I also had the opportunity to tour St. Peter's Basilica, see Michelangelo's Sistine Chapel, and climb the Spanish Steps.

From Rome I traveled to Paris where, staying on a college campus, I participated in the 1961 Quadrennial Meeting of the International Society of Soil Mechanics and Foundation Engineering. The technical aspects of the meeting were outstanding, as were the social events. The closing event was a dinner held at the Palace of Versailles, where I remember being struck by the fact that each place setting had seven glasses. I can remember using only five—for water, red wine, white wine, champagne, and cognac.

Following Paris I took a boat across the English Channel to England and a train to London and then to the home of a former fellow Purdue graduate student and her husband. I stayed with them for three weeks. During each week I would visit British universities to learn of their research activities in the area of soil mechanics and foundation engineering. During each weekend I would enjoy their companionship and the hospitality of their home.

It was a grand and educational nine weeks in Europe, capping off several long years of my graduate education.

FIVE

Blueprint for a Career;
Blueprint for a Life

M Y RETURN from Europe left me ready and desirous to start working in the private sector. But still, despite my experience, my education, and my ambition, I received no job offers.

I did receive a call from my old friend Dr. John Shupe, however. John and I had been fellow graduate students at Purdue University. He completed his doctoral studies a year before I received my PhD and had since become the assistant dean of engineering at Kansas State University. John called to ask me if I would be interested in a position as assistant professor at Kansas State. Lacking any private sector job offers, I interviewed for the opening and was hired for the job. In 1961 I packed up my car and drove to Manhattan, Kansas, to begin my teaching duties at Kansas State's Department of Civil Engineering.

It wasn't long after I arrived in Kansas that I once again was met by Jim Crow. Shortly after I showed up in Manhattan I needed a haircut and randomly chose a downtown barbershop. The barber gave me a good haircut, and I kept returning. One day when I returned, however, he told me he could no longer cut my hair. It turned out that some of his other customers complained about my presence and indicated that unless he stopped serving me, they would not return. This made me angry. I ended up writing a letter to the editor of the local newspaper, essentially pointing out that while the community thought I was good enough to teach their kids, I apparently was not good enough to get a haircut from a white barber in town. This created a stir on campus. Students organized protest marches, without extending the courtesy of even consulting me for my support. Nevertheless, their efforts proved effective, because the barber got a message to me that I would be welcomed in his shop. I returned, and he cut my hair for the remainder of my tenure at K-State.

Haircut troubles aside, my first year at K-State went well. We had a great faculty group who got along well and worked well together. My teaching consisted of courses in soil mechanics and foundation engineering and airport and highway pavement design. I had been there less than a year, however, when I was contacted by Dr. Eugene Zwoyer, who was then head of the US Air Force Shock Tube Facility in Albuquerque, New Mexico. I had met Gene and his wife, Dorothy, through the American Society of Civil Engineers back when he was the society's executive director. The head of soil dynamics research at Gene's facility wanted to return to the University of California to complete work on his doctorate, and Gene needed someone to assume his duties for the period of his absence, one academic year. I felt this was a unique opportunity, an extension of the work I did for my master's degree, and afforded the possibility for research funding once I returned to K-State. I broached the subject with the head of my department at K-State and, he agreed. Thus, at the end of the 1961–62 school year, I packed up my car and drove to Albuquerque to become the interim head of soil mechanics research at that facility.

Gene Zwoyer had assembled an outstanding group of people at the facility. The work was interesting and challenging. It was a thrill to be associated, again, with an outstanding group of professionals who worked hard and played hard. Gene and Dorothy Zwoyer hosted some of the best parties I have ever attended.

Nevertheless, social life in Albuquerque was not always color blind. A member of our team, Dr. Barry Donovan, brought a young lady who happened to be the sister of the wife of one of my fellow employees to one of the Zwoyer's parties. At the time, the Twist was the dance craze. Barry could not dance, so his date and I danced the night away. Toward the end of the evening, I asked to take her out on a dinner date and she said yes. On the evening of the date, I drove to her sister's home to pick her up. I was invited in, seated, and told that she was not there. I got up and left. It was obvious that they did not want me to date her.

On another occasion, our staff was invited to Vicksburg, Mississippi, to exchange nuclear weapons effect research knowledge with the US Army Corps of Engineers. As head of soil dynamics research for the facility, I had a duty and a right to attend, and should have attended that meeting. I was told I could not go, however, because there was no place for a black man to stay in Vicksburg. I protested, but to no avail. I even wrote to President John F. Kennedy, who claimed to be a champion of civil rights, asking him to intervene, but he did not.

My frustration with racism everywhere I went was soon dulled a bit by something much stronger: Love.

In the spring of 1963, my friends from Prairie View A & M, Professors Pearl and Edward Martin, invited me to be their guest at an Alpha Kappa Alpha Sorority formal dinner dance to be held in their hometown. They promised to get me a date. I accepted and on the appropriate day returned to Prairie View. Shortly after my arrival they took me to the home of their dear friends Herman T. and Gwendolyn B. Jones. They wanted to introduce me to their friends, but more importantly, they wanted to introduce me to their friends' daughter, Janet Jones. Janet was to be my date for the dinner dance.

Janet Jones was—and still is—bright, intelligent, articulate, and attractive. She and I hit it off immediately and I was impressed by the warmth and the hospitality that both she and her entire family showed me that night in Prairie View. It marked the beginning of a lifelong relationship that would eventually lead to marriage.

After my year in Albuquerque, I drove back to Manhattan to resume my teaching position at K-State at the start of the 1963–64 academic year. Upon arriving, though, I discovered that my former department chair had retired and that his replacement did not like the fact that I had spent the previous year on leave. It wasn't long before it was clear that he could not get over his displeasure with me. Later in the school year, he recommended a fellow faculty member who was less qualified than I for promotion to the rank of associate professor. The writing was clearly on the wall. I had no future at K-State.

About that time Dr. Ernest Selig, a good friend and outstanding geotechnical engineer, let me know that he had a key position open at the Illinois Institute of Technology (IIT) Research Institute in Chicago. He had his superior, Dr. Eben Vey, offer me a position to work in his group. Recognizing the limited opportunities I would have at K-State, I accepted the offer and prepared to move back to Chicago.

Once again I found myself leaving a place with mixed feelings. I carried memories warmed by good friends, supportive mentors, and work that gave me a sense of accomplishment. I also carried memories of sadness and disappointment caused once again by the specter of Jim Crow racism.

At the end of the spring semester 1964, I packed up and drove to Chicago to begin work at the Illinois Institute of Technology Research Institute. It felt good to be going home and knowing I would be close to my mother, sister, and friends again.

*   *   *

I moved into a furnished apartment on the IIT campus. Conveniently, it was about a half-hour drive from my mother's home, which let me take advantage of her loving attention and good home cooking once again.

The work at the IIT Research Institute was interesting and challenging, and I worked with a great group of guys. Dr. Vey and his deputy, Dr. Selig, who led our geotechnical engineering group, were excellent engineers. They also were good managers who would give me and others in my group a research assignment and then get out of the way, letting us do the research we needed to do.

At IIT I was able to continue the research work that I started at Purdue University and at the US Air Force Shock Tube Facility. My research focused mostly on stress wave propagation though soils, as well as air field pavement evaluation. This work led to another area of specialized research that focused on aircraft tire–soil interactions during landings, which took me and my colleagues Bill Truesdale and John Anderson to Langley Air Force Base in Virginia for research. At one point during our study, Bill and John wanted to return to Chicago to take the professional engineers' examination. I was to remain at Langley in their absence.

There was a problem, however. This was the 1960s, and the white construction contractor on the Langley project did not want to work directly under the supervision of a black engineer. There was no reason I shouldn't direct the project, but Bill and John begged me to agree not to direct the contractor during their absence. Instead, I was only to observe and report on his performance. If any work had to be redone, they said, they would direct the contractor to do so upon their return. I agreed to Bill and John's wishes, but it was not one of my shining moments, and was one that I came to regret. Evidently I was more concerned about the two of them than I was about standing up for my own rights.

Upon returning to Chicago I became involved in professional and technical activities, especially in the local chapter of the American Society of Civil Engineers, and particularly its geotechnical engineering group. There, I met three people who proved to be very important for my future: John P. Gnaedinger and Clyde N. Baker Jr., principals in the firm known as Soil Testing Services Inc., and David Novick, principal in the firm of Westerhoff and Novick.

My social life in Chicago revolved around two distinct groups that reached back to my college days: one was a local group of fraternity brothers; the other was a group of friends I met through Dr. Jim Bucker and Jean Anne Pierce Durades, whom I had met while we all attended the University of Illinois. We did a lot together, but we especially gravitated toward bridge and skiing.

The first ski trip I made with the group was to Mont-Tremblant in Canada. The first day was miserable. If I had been closer to home, I would have said to hell with skiing and left. But I was stuck in Canada for a week. And by the end of the week, I was hooked on the sport, and still am today. After Canada, our next trip was to Vail, Colorado, which back then was only getting started. All of us were enamored with Vail. I tried to get Jim Buckner and others in our group to join me in purchasing a condominium in Vail. We looked at properties and the one we liked best was the penthouse at the Mountain Haus, which was directly across from the gondola that took skiers to the top of the mountain. We could have purchased it for $90,000 in the spring of 1961, shortly after the resort opened. But my friends were not interested, and they felt the price would come down. Today that property is worth well over $1 million.

Our group skied at most of the major resorts in the United States west of the Mississippi River, but the best day of skiing I ever had was at Sun Valley, Idaho. My friend Jim Buckner had left a day before me and I was skiing alone and happened to ride up the ski lift with a young lady, a native, who asked me if I would like to ski with her. I readily accepted. The sun was shining, the weather was pleasant, she was a great skier, and we had a ball. Afterward she took me by her home and introduced me to her family and we had lunch. It was a wonderful day.

We didn't just ski North America. At the time, the Chicago Metropolitan Ski Council took trips to places where Americans did not normally ski. We joined them on trips to Norway and what was then known as Czechoslovakia, which, outside of touring, were busts. It rained continuously during our stay in Norway. In Czechoslovakia the sun was shining but the snow conditions were lousy. So in both countries we spent most of our time touring instead of skiing.

Some of us made a side trip to Austria immediately upon our arrival in Czechoslovakia. In Vienna, we spent the night and dined at the unique and classic Hotel Sacher, where the Sacher-Torte was created. The next day we stopped at the Austrian–Czechoslovakian border to go through customs. One of the men in our group had a pencil-thin moustache, which he had grown subsequent to having his passport picture taken. The border guards refused to let us into Czechoslovakia until he shaved it off. After we sat there for over two hours, he reluctantly shaved and we went on our way. We proceeded back to Prague, which I shall always remember for its wonderful sights and great people, and for the dinner we had on the top floor of a hotel, which afforded a beautiful view of the city.

Back home, bridge continued to be a favorite pastime. We played cards biweekly at a minimum. One member of the group would host the game and we rotated hosting. Along with me, there was Nelson Brown, a lawyer; Hank Wiggins, a physician; and Jim Buckner, a dentist. When I hosted, it was at the faculty club at IIT. Mostly, though, we played at Nelson's home in Hyde Park. Even after I later moved to Washington, DC, the sessions continued whenever I returned to Chicago. We would normally meet at noon, play bridge, break to eat dinner (usually barbeque ribs), and resume playing. We would continue playing into late evening.

Nelson was a great guy and a wonderful friend. Unfortunately, his family had been star-crossed and prone to tragedy. Back in 1967, when our group was planning a ski trip to Vail, I got a call from Nelson requesting that I cancel his family's accommodations for the trip. It turns out his sister, Donna Branion, had been found murdered in her home. That night Nelson called and requested that I try to get their rooms back. His brother-in-law, John Branion, felt it would be good to get his children out of the house where their mother had been killed. This made good sense to me and I was able to revive their reservations. Nelson's brother-in-law and his family joined us and remained for the duration of our trip. But later his brother-in-law became a "person of interest" in the murder of his wife. His joining us on the trip to Vail during this critical time was used by the Chicago Police Department and the Chicago Defender Newspaper to turn the public against him and eventually to get him convicted of murder. Sixteen years later, tragedy struck the Brown family once again—this time it hit even closer to home. One Sunday evening Nelson returned to his law offices on Chicago's South Side. Later he was found dead in front of his office door, with his key stuck in the door lock and a knife stuck in his neck. The police designated it a murder–robbery. Nelson was the unofficial leader of our bridge group and his horrific death broke up our old gang. I remain close only to Jim Buckner and Jean Ann Durades. Since Nelson's funeral, I have not seen any of the others, except Sonia Brown and "Teesee" Hooks. If Nelson had lived, I'm sure our social lives would have been very different.

The 1960s, of course, were some of the most tumultuous times in US history, and Chicago was not immune to the upheaval that roiled the country. In 1966 Dr. Martin Luther King Jr. came to Chicago, leading marches through all-white neighborhoods to try to end housing discrimination. Two years later the Democratic National Convention in Chicago would explode in violence and riots that left parts of the city's South Side burned and looted, and protesters bloody and beaten on Michigan Avenue.

Amid all this turmoil I continued the long-distance relationship with the woman I had fallen in love with back in Prairie View, Texas, Janet Jones. After several years of our cross-state courtship, I traveled to Texas to ask Jan's father for her hand in marriage. He gave his blessing.

Our wedding at the St. Martin de Porres Church in September 1967 was a grand affair. My family and closest friends from Chicago traveled to Prairie View, Texas. We were housed in one of the university's dormitories and, since school was out, we had the place all to ourselves. We "partied hearty" every night before the wedding until the wee hours of the morning. That prelude to the wedding reminded me of the musical *My Fair Lady* and the scene where the father of Eliza Doolittle sang, "Get me to the church on time." Jan and I spent the night of our marriage in a hotel in Houston, and the next day we flew to Puerto Rico for our honeymoon.

My personal and my professional life were at a new apex. My career was blossoming; my expertise and my reputation in geotechnical engineering were growing. And now, I was married and inching my way toward settling down.

A year later, I would reach another turning point in my life that would uproot me from my Chicago home and take me to the place that I call home today.

Six

Tangents and Turning Points

FOLLOWING A wonderful honeymoon in Puerto Rico, Jan and I returned to Chicago and began our life together as newlyweds. Jan did not know Chicago well, and my mother's home was in a neighborhood that was daunting for a young woman brought up on a college campus. As a result, Jan and my family had little contact without me. Furthermore, since we were living in a furnished apartment, there was not much Jan could do with our living space. So while I was off doing research, Jan filled her days working on a volunteer project, looking for household furnishings, and enjoying Chicago's rich cultural venues. In her own unique manner, Jan was able to quickly develop some lifelong friends in Chicago.

Overall, though, it wasn't exactly a comfortable start to a new life for Jan in Chicago. So it's not surprising that she was happy when I decided in 1968 to take a teaching job at Howard University in Washington, DC, a place she knew from visiting her sister and brother-in-law and their children, who lived there.

I had met the chairman of Howard University's Department of Civil Engineering, Dr. Walter T. Daniels, at a conference. Ever since our initial meeting, he had been after me to become a member of his faculty at Howard University. With my work at the IIT Research Institute slowing down, I began to consider his entreaties. Finally, I made the decision to accept his offer and join the faculty at Howard University's Department of Civil Engineering.

On the way to Washington, while driving on the Pennsylvania Turnpike, our car broke down. Fortunately we were able to drive it long enough to get off the turnpike and to a motel, where we spent the night. The next morning I called a Volkswagen dealer. He came and picked us up in his car and took us to his dealership, where we were able to purchase a new Volkswagen. The following day we continued on to Washington—a newly married couple in a new car, off to a new city and a new career.

We weren't long in Washington, however, when the city—and seemingly the entire country—went crazy. Just weeks after our arrival, Dr. Martin Luther King

Jr. was shot dead in Memphis while he and others were planning a march in support of the city's black garbage workers, who were on strike for higher wages. Ironically, Dr. King was scheduled to be in Atlanta participating in a poor peoples' march but, instead, decided to support the effort in Memphis on that fateful day. At the time, we were living in Southwest DC, near the residence of Hubert Humphrey. Because of its proximity we were surrounded by armed reservists. The lobby doors to our apartment were locked and the nearby Safeway store had armed soldiers lined up in front of it.

Days later, US Secretary of Defense Clark Clifford called up 24,500 military reservists to aid the growing war in Vietnam, which suddenly added additional stress for me and my new wife and our life. Earlier that same year I had enlisted in the US Naval Reserve. While at the University of Illinois I had been impressed with the students who were in the Navy ROTC. I had also taken up sailing and I enjoyed the water, making the Naval Reserve even more attractive to me. In Washington I reported for my monthly training with the construction battalion, where I served as the personnel officer. But fortunately I was not called to active duty.

In time, Washington and the world began to settle down, and so did we. Jan launched into furnishing our new home and getting better acquainted with the city. Our social life revolved principally around our friends Vincent and Diane Cohen, our neighbors across the hall, and our relatives, the Lewises. We also shared a social life with Carl and Dorothy Hampton and Earl and Estelle Greenfield.

At Howard, my career was in full swing, and Washington began to feel like home. Professor Daniels kept the promises he made while recruiting me and gave me a budget ample enough to design and equip a first-class soil mechanics laboratory. A friend, Dr. Anwar Wissa, who worked for a soil and rock testing equipment manufacturer, assisted me in this effort, as did my laboratory technician, the late William B. Steward. Anwar helped to design the laboratory and provided directions and instructions on the operation of the purchased equipment to William and me. By the end of my first year at Howard, the new laboratory was in operation. Also by then I had a research contract with the US Forest Service to study the soils and rocks of an area called the Idaho Batholith, which straddles portions of the states of Idaho and Montana. The purpose of the study was to gain information that would permit the building of more stable roads through that area.

That summer one of my graduate students, Norman Ng-A-Qui, and I set out for the area to collect soil and rock samples for study back at Howard. The collection sites were many miles away from town. One day while we were at that site, I lost the car keys while scrambling over the mountain slopes collecting samples. What to do? I could have sat down and let Norman walk back to town to get a new set of keys from the rental car agency. However, I decided that since I was the one who caused the problem, I should solve it. I began the long walk back to the nearest town. Fortunately, shortly after I reached the highway, a car came along and gave me a lift to the rental car agency. It was a day wasted but it taught me a lesson: Be more careful!

The US Department of Agriculture's Forest Service controls most of the Idaho Batholith. The agency was concerned about soil and rock slope instability in the area and wanted to learn more about their characteristics in order to minimize damage and potential injury and death to people and property in the area. It was an interesting and challenging assignment. In addition, I had an opportunity to observe the hard work and dedication of Forest Service personnel. I came away deeply impressed by it and especially grateful for the support that Dr. Walter Meganan and his staff provided me, which helped to improve the quality of the research we produced. Once I got back to Washington, Norman and I began preparing the samples for testing and testing them. Following completion of the data collection and analysis, I submitted my report to the USDA Forest Service and published a paper based on the results.

The engineering faculty at Howard University were excellent. They were great teachers, and those who were so inclined were great researchers as well. My only hang-up was the management style of the dean of engineering, who believed in managing with an iron fist and imposing tight controls. We often had verbal confrontations during faculty meetings because he treated his faculty members like children. The relationships with the rest of my colleagues and students at Howard, however, resulted in lasting friendships and collaborations. One of my former students, James Johnson, went on to receive a doctorate, returned to the Howard University faculty, and rose to the position of dean of engineering. Other former students of mine are now CEOs of independent design and/or program and construction management firms.

It was while I was teaching at Howard that I met a US Army Corps of Engineers officer stationed in the Washington area who had developed a consulting practice. When he learned that he was being transferred to a different locality, he asked if I would like to take over his practice when he left. I agreed. After some indoctrination and introductions to his clients,

he departed and I assumed his responsibilities. Most of
his work was with one firm. Subsequently, I provided
all the needed consulting services while continuing my
teaching and research duties at Howard University. I
did other consulting work while at Howard as well.
One year, Richard (Dick) Woodward, co-founder of
the geotechnical engineering firm Woodward, Clyde
& Associates, offered me a summer job in his firm's
main office in Oakland, California. I accepted and
spent an interesting and challenging summer working
with that firm. I also spent a summer working with my
old Chicago friends at Gnaedinger and Baker while
Clyde was away on vacation. I benefitted substantially
from that professionally rewarding experience. During that time, I also had the pleasure of staying in the
home of Clyde and his lovely wife, Jeannette, while
they vacationed in New England.

It wasn't entirely surprising, then, when one day I
received a call from John and Clyde that would once
again take my life and career on a tangent. At that
time, one could not practice engineering in the District
of Columbia as a corporation. It had to be done as a
partnership. John and Clyde asked me if I would join
them in a partnership to practice geotechnical engineering in the District of Columbia. I readily agreed.
In 1971, we formed the firm of Gnaedinger, Baker,

Hampton and Associates (GBH), with me having majority interest and as its president. Clyde and John taught me how to manage the business, and over time the firm prospered.

I am indebted to both John and Clyde for the teaching, guidance, and assistance they gave me in the early stages of my consulting career. Under them and other mentors, I learned that running an engineering business isn't only about the engineering work. They taught me about the value of client relations, and how important it is to keep clients informed, involved, and happy throughout a project. They put me on the right path for business success and for that I shall be eternally grateful.

John Gnaedinger, Clyde Baker, and Dick Woodward are all people I met through participation in professional and technical activities and were some of the role models that helped shape the rest of my career. Another one would come into my life one night at the Gaslight Club on Sixteenth Street in Washington, when he and his dining partner, A. James Clark, chairman and CEO of the construction company Clark Enterprises Inc., invited Jan and me to join them at their table. Our decision to join them proved to be one of the most fortuitous of my life.

James A. Caywood was then president of De Leuw, Cather & Company, a consulting engineering firm that specialized in transportation planning and design. A few weeks after Jan and I joined him for dinner that night at the Gaslight Club, he invited me to lunch. I accepted. During lunch he indicated that the Washington Metropolitan Area Transit Authority (WMATA) would be building a new rail transit system in Washington, DC. He suggested that it would be a great time for me to start a business in order to seek some of that work. I went home, thought about what he said, and concluded that he was right. I sold my interest in GBH to John and Clyde and struck out on my own, with little planning but with confidence in the wisdom and vision of my newfound friend and soon-to-be mentor, Jim Caywood. Exactly why I put so much trust and faith into Jim at the time, I do not know. But it was well placed.

In January 1973, Delon Hampton & Associates (DHA) Chartered was incorporated in the District of Columbia. While I started the firm and it carries my name, without the vision and support of that wise Kentucky gentleman, Jim Caywood, DHA would not exist. Conceptually, DHA was Jim's idea and he worked hard on my behalf without compensation to help make DHA a success. Unfortunately, I do not believe I ever said "thanks a million" to Jim before he passed away, but I hope he knew how much I appreciated his counsel, guidance, friendship, and vision. I hope he is looking down upon us and is pleased with DHA and the key role he played in creating it.

Ironically, it almost never came to pass that Jim and I would work together on the project he first approached me about. Jim had asked me to join his team seeking the WMATA general engineering and architectural consulting contract. However, by the time he asked me, I had already committed to being on another team and felt honor bound by that commitment. Jim respected my decision to honor my commitment to the other team. But after his team won the contract, he invited DHA to join his team. We had been competitors; now we were partners. He understood the ethics of my position and had forgiven me.

Jim Caywood, like John Gnaedinger, Clyde Baker, and Dick Woodward, was a unique individual who not only believed in equal opportunity but also practiced it. Unfortunately, those who followed Jim as leaders of the firm he led did not demonstrate the same commitment. I believe that the leadership he left behind in his firm were jealous of my special relationship with Jim and/or did not believe in affirmative action, so when Jim retired DHA's special relationship with that firm ceased.

My mother, Elizabeth Lewis Hampton, me, and my oldest sister, Vera, ca. 1960.

Raymond D. Douglas, MD. Uncle Raymond was a mentor to my brother, Clarence, and active in Texas state politics.

Me with my brother Clarence just before Jan and I got married, 1967.

My first wife, Jan, me, and my mother, Elizabeth, on our wedding day.

My wife, Sonia, at the City Club in Washington, DC, on our wedding day.

Left top: Jan and me at home with friends. Graduate school roommate and friend Henry Moses at back.

Left bottom: I met my second wife, Fay, on a flight from Washington to Chicago.

Dr. Ralph B. Peck, a great geotechnical engineer and my inspiring professor at the University of Illinois.

Purdue professor Gerald A. Leonards, who offered me a half-time teaching assistantship in his area of soil mechanics and foundation engineering, which enhanced my knowledge of the subject.

My doctoral advisor at Purdue, Professor Eldon Yoder.

My fellow Purdue graduate student Milton Harr taught me to appreciate classical music, fine art, and fine wine . . . as well as encouraging my enthusiasm for geotechnical engineering and the Russian language.

With some of my favorite University of Illinois professors (*left to right*): David Daniel, John D. Haltiwanger, Narbey Khachaturian, and William Hall.

My mentors and partners in GBH, John Gnaedinger and Clyde Baker Jr.

Above: Opening the DHA office in Silver Spring, Maryland. *Left to right*: Dr. R. Varadarajan, Montgomery County Executive Charles Gilchrist, and me.

Right top: My friend and mentor Jim Caywood, standing with wife Carol, being honored at a National Society of Black Engineers' dinner. Secretary of Transportation Coleman is seated in the center.

Right bottom: Meeting with Secretary of Transportation William T. Coleman in the late 1970s as part of a delegation of the National Society of Black Engineers.

I was proud that DHA was part of construction management team building the new US Capitol Visitor Center. Here I am in 2003 with DHA colleague Elijah Rogers, Keith Valdez, and a colleague from the Gilbane construction company.

Left top: Me with COO Elijah B. Rogers, long-term assistant Deborah Horn, and head of business development John M. Zimmer at DHA's thirtieth anniversary reception.

Left bottom: Signing the Southern California Rapid Transit District contact, a big breakthrough for DHA. I am with (left to right) David Hammond, John Dyer, and Robert Murray.

DHA provided civil and structural engineering and support for the $350 million Gallery Place development, which was a particular challenge because of its constrained site in the middle of downtown Washington, atop and adjacent to one of the busiest stations in the Washington Metro system.

Left top: Washington DC's Dulles International Airport has been a core project for DHA for over 20 years.

Left bottom: Not glamorous, but you'd notice if it was not there! The Atlanta West Combined Sewer Overflow.

Delon and Sonia stepping down as President and First Lady of the American Society of Civil Engineers (ASCE).

Right top: At ASCE I created the Outstanding Projects and Leaders awards (OPAL). Here I am with the first award winners: Eugene J. Fasullo, Steve Bechtel, Albert A. Dorman, and T. Y. Lin.

Right bottom: Then ASCE Executive Director Edward Pfrang and I meeting with Chilean President Eduardo Frei Ruiz-Tagle.

Receiving a certificate from Secretary of Commerce William M. Daley for my service on the Malcolm Baldridge National Quality Award Committee in 1999.

Left top: Presenting the Hoover Medal Award for major contributions to engineering to President Jimmy Carter.

Left bottom: Greeting then Secretary of Transportation Rodney E. Slater at a Center for National Policy meeting.

The National Society of Black Engineers awarded me the Golden Torch Award in 2005. My dear friend Pat Natale, executive director of ASCE, presented it.

Good fun with fellow members of the American Consulting Engineers Council/Metropolitan Washington Chapter during the ACEC annual convention.

Unveiling the portrait of my mother, Elizabeth, and myself that hangs in the lobby of the Delon and Elizabeth Hampton Hall of Civil Engineering at Purdue University.

Left top: At the dedication of the Delon and Elizabeth Hampton Hall of Civil Engineering at Purdue University, my gift back to the world of education, September 14, 2012.

Left bottom: With Sonia receiving the 2012 Distinguished Pinnacle Award from Purdue's Acting President, Timothy D. Sands and Dean of the College of Engineering, Leah H. Jamieson.

Overall, the life I have constructed has been a wonderful life—one that has given me the opportunity to serve my family, my country, and my profession. To all who contributed to my success and happiness, thanks a million.

SEVEN

Building a Business

WHEN I told John Gnaedinger of my plans to leave GBH and to start my own firm with a broader mandate, he was not pleased. However, we parted on good terms and Gnaedinger and Baker in fact initially owned a part of DHA. While we were indeed partners in this company, I was beginning to feel that our partnership was sending mixed messages. It seemed that some people were looking at DHA as a possible front for securing minority set-aside contracts with me as a figurehead and Gnaedinger and Baker in actual control.

Even though this was not the case, Clyde and John agreed to a buyout and we moved forward. John never believed I gave him and Clyde the credit they deserved for my success. That's simply not true. In conversations, speeches, and writings I have always expressed gratitude for John and Clyde's role in my private sector success, and I continue to do so. They taught me how to manage. Without their mentoring help, DHA would not be where it is today.

DHA's first office was located in the 1500 block of New Hampshire Avenue NW in Washington. My first hire was Jan's cousin, Stephanie (Rigney) Roberts. Stephanie had recently married and moved to the Washington, DC, area from her family home in Kansas City. She and I worked well together and she grew within our organization from secretary to the position of vice president for administration.

My second employee was Dr. R. Varadarajan ("Rajan"). He was the first engineer I hired. Rajan played a vital role in the development of DHA. Through hard work and dedication he rose to the position of chief engineer and later to principal in the firm. Rajan was an outstanding engineer and contributed greatly to the development of DHA. He wanted to be our chief operating officer, but at the time I decided to hire one. I just didn't feel he had the skills necessary for the job. Shortly after Elijah B. Rogers came on board as our COO, Rajan left and started his own firm. Had he seen that his true talents were in engineering and not in corporate management, DHA would not have lost his talents and both he and DHA would have benefitted.

An office and a couple of employees, we quickly realized, does not make a viable, growing business. Especially in a field dominated by well-established, mega engineering firms, we knew we had to prove ourselves to the decision makers who counted. Once again, my friend and mentor Jim Caywood stepped up. He convinced Vernon Garrett, WMATA's chief engineer and one of the most important decision makers in the metro system's expansion plans, to meet with me and my staff in order to assess our engineering capabilities. When Vern came to our office, he saw three people: Stephanie, Rajan, and me. Despite our small size, we were able to convince him we had the engineering and management skills WMATA wanted and needed.

At Jim's advice, I invited the bigger firm of Chicago-based Westenhoff and Novick to join DHA to seek a contract with WMATA for the design of two rail service and inspection shops. I had known David Novick, the firm's CEO, from my prior tenure with the Illinois Institute of Technology (IIT) Research Institute. After I met with him again to discuss the WMATA contract, we agreed to become joint venture partners, with DHA as the managing partner. That was a big concession on Dave's part since his firm was a major player in the engineering profession and DHA had yet to receive its first contract.

Together we submitted qualifications and competed for design of the two rail car service and inspection shops—the Huntington-Springfield and West Falls Church shops. We got shortlisted, made our presentation, and remarkably, we won.

The constructed value of the contract—DHA's first—was about $40 million. But winning the contract to design the two commuter rail service and inspection shops was much more valuable than that. WMATA showed a lot of guts in giving our team that assignment. If we had failed, those who had made the selection probably would have been severely criticized for awarding that assignment to a team led by a firm with no prior history. WMATA had faith in our small, minority-owned firm, and I shall forever be thankful for that.

WMATA's gamble paid off for the rail authority, but it also paid off big for us. It helped establish our reputation for quality work on major design projects, and it allowed us to use the WMATA "seal of approval" to help win major heavy rail transit projects around the nation. From Washington, we went on to Atlanta, then Miami, then Houston, then Los Angeles and beyond, where we have been fortunate to win major contracts for the design of major segments of heavy rail transit as the prime and/or major sub-consultant.

If not for that first win from WMATA back in the 1970s, we could not have had the experience—nor the success—we've had.

But before DHA could succeed, it had to survive.

The celebration over the WMATA contract quickly turned to concern. We were scheduled to begin work on the two rail service and inspection shops in July 1973, but unfortunately we did not get the notice to proceed until March 1974. This caused DHA a substantial financial hardship.

Fortunately we were able to win some additional work in the interim that would help shape the firm's future. The principal job we won was another Washington-area contract, this one with the Federal Aviation Administration to design the rehabilitation of an apron and adjacent taxiway at the Washington National Airport, now known as Ronald Reagan Washington National Airport. Subsequently we were also able to win research contracts from the Federal Highway Administration and the Urban Mass Transit Administration (now the Federal Transit Administration), which helped us through this tough period. DHA is deeply grateful to Dr. Don A. Linger, formerly of the FHWA Office of Research, and Gilbert Butler, a member of the then Urban Mass Transit Administrations (now FTA), for selecting DHA to provide research services during that critical time. At the time, DHA was in the federal government's minority business program, so their organizations could make those selections.

Yet despite the additional work we were racking up, cash flow was still a problem. Fortunately I had my salary from teaching at Howard University that was helping sustain the young company, but what I needed was a line of credit. Unfortunately, though, no bank would advance DHA a loan or give us a line of credit. One night I was at a reception and ran into my friend Ron Steele, who inquired about DHA's progress. I told him things were moving along satisfactorily except that I was having difficulty obtaining bank financing. A few weeks later I got a call from Ron's banker at American Security and Trust Bank, who indicated that Ron had mentioned I might need banking assistance. I met with him and the result was a $5,000 loan. What I really wanted was a line of credit, but I didn't turn down the loan—I couldn't afford to.

My banker and I continued to work together. With his support, I applied to the US Small Business Administration (SBA) for a $25,000 loan guarantee, and—after some explaining to the SBA representative about basic business operations and finance—we eventually received the loan guarantee. It took some time to get that approval, however. While waiting for it, I still needed additional financial help to make the payroll and keep my young company running. I turned to my brother Clarence, who by then was a wealthy physician. But instead of lending me money, he put me in touch with his local banker in Belle Plaine, Iowa, who gave me a loan. Although I was initially surprised that Clarence did not give me the loan I had requested, I later understood. Friends and relatives, in general, do not have a strong tendency to repay loans made to them by friends and/or relatives. I have been burned several times by failing to recognize that tendency. Having lent money to friends and relatives and not been repaid, I learned my lesson and I no longer lend money to anyone.

As anyone who has ever started a small business knows, I quickly learned that making payroll, keeping revenues coming, and finding financing to fill in when needed is crucial. Fortunately, between the two bank loans and my personal finances, DHA was able to survive its financial crisis and get over a critical hump.

While I was struggling to build the business and keep the finances in order, DHA was beginning to build a reputation for itself that began to extend outside the Washington area. Our work on the WMATA rail service and inspection shops was getting some notice among other rail authorities. Our work at Ronald Reagan Washington National gave us the experience to begin bidding on other airport work. And our contracts with the FHWA started to open up new business for us on street, highway, and bridge work.

DHA also was a beneficiary of the times.

For instance, the year DHA was founded, 1973, was also the year that Congress passed the Federal-Aid Highway Act, which for the first time permitted states to use federal Highway Trust Fund money for mass transit. As a result, new rail engineering and construction work began to open up in states all across the country during DHA's formative years.

In 1978 came the Airline Deregulation Act, which opened up commercial air travel to the masses, resulting in rapid expansion in the airline industry—which ultimately resulted in more airports needing more engineering and construction work to expand and meet growing demand from airlines and travelers.

And the Civil Rights Act of 1964, and subsequently the Voting Rights Act of 1965, ultimately opened up more opportunities for African-Americans, making it more socially unacceptable, at least, to discriminate against minorities in business. Advances in affirmative action, equal opportunity, and minority contracting laws that were created or solidified by the courts in the early 1970s, meanwhile, created new opportunities for minority contractors on government projects at both the state and federal levels.

Our work both inside and outside of Washington began to grow, especially after we added program management and construction management services to our firm's capabilities in the 1980s.

In my hometown of Chicago, we designed the Archer Avenue heavy rail transit station and connecting rail line segments and provided, as part of a team, construction management support services on the rail line constructed between downtown Chicago and O'Hare International Airport. We also designed, as prime consultant, a major segment of the City of Chicago's Tunnel and Reservoir Project ("Deep Tunnel"), provided structural design for the renovation of sky boxes at Soldiers Field, and provided civil and structural design services, as well as construction inspection services, for the new Comiskey Park, among other projects.

We branched out to Houston after we were awarded prime and/or major sub-consultant contracts for the design of major segments of a heavy rail system there. It was going well until the contract was terminated after only about 30 percent of the design work was done, when a referendum to fund the project was defeated.

In Atlanta, we won a contract to provide structural engineering design services for the proposed Omni Rail Transit Station to be built by MARTA.

Thanks to those first rail projects awarded to us by WMATA, DHA was growing, and growing fast.

One day I received a call in my office from a man who asked if I would be interested in meeting his client to explore a possible working relationship. I replied affirmatively. He then asked that I call him prior to my next visit to Atlanta and said that upon my arrival he would take me to meet his client. I agreed. I called him after I scheduled my next trip to Atlanta, where we were doing work on MARTA's proposed Omni Station, which today serves landmarks such as the Georgia Dome, the Georgia World Congress Center, and the CNN Center. He met me at the airport and took me to the office of Jordan, Jones and Goulding (JJ&G), a prominent Atlanta-based firm, where I met with William Jordan, Charles Jones, and Randolph Goulding, the principals of the firm. The net result was an agreement that we would work together to seek contracts for design and construction management and supervision of major water and wastewater treatment facilities and conveyance systems in Atlanta and the State of Georgia. This venture proved successful over many years. Our most recent contract done in joint venture with JJ&G

and Hatch, Mott, MacDonald involved the design and construction oversight of the West Combined Sewer Overflow Facility, which is now serving the needs of the citizens of metropolitan Atlanta. Our transit and water and wastewater projects in the Atlanta region led to our establishing an office in Atlanta which still exists.

Our original effort as sub-consultant to JJ&G was to provide civil and structural support for the design of the Constitution Road Combined Sewer Overflow Facility. Subsequently we provided JJ&G with civil and structural engineering support for major water and wastewater facilities in Georgia for the cities of Atlanta and Macon, Fulton County, and other municipalities. Our largest job with the firm was performed in joint venture with JJ&G and the firm Mott McDonald for the West CSO Tunnel Design and Construction Project.

Charlie Jones and his wife, Judy, became great friends of my wife, Sonia, and me. We travelled the world together having much fun. One of my most cherished memories is of Judy on stage at the Gaslight Club in Washington, DC, singing, "I'm a Rambling Wreck from Georgia Tech," with Charlie, their daughter, Carol, and me cheering her on. Another is of Judy riding a camel when we all took a trip together to Morocco.

Unfortunately Judy died years ago, a tragedy from which Charlie has never fully recovered. Over the years, often when I visited Atlanta I invited Charlie for dinner at Bones, a restaurant that was long our favorite meeting spot. In recent years, though, he has joined me for dinner only once. We had fun and reminisced about the good times the four of us had together, but maybe Bones brought back too many memories of Judy for him.

One evening Charlie's daughter-in-law, Stephanie Jones, called me and told me if I wanted to have dinner with Charlie during my next trip to Atlanta, she would arrange it. I thanked her profusely. Shortly thereafter I called Stephanie and we scheduled dinner. I was filled with joy. I had my Charlie back! The day the dinner was to take place we had a terrible storm in the Washington, DC, area and my plane had over a five hour delayed takeoff—three hours were spent sitting in a plane on a tarmac. The delay was worth it. Charlie and I had a wonderful time, mixed with laughter and tears.

I am very grateful to Stephanie for getting us together, and I am looking forward to my next visit to Atlanta.

From Atlanta, DHA pushed even further south, to Florida. Elijah B. Rogers, DHA's chief operating officer at the time, was a native of Orlando. He felt that if we could get a foothold in that booming state, we could have a profitable office. We won a contract, rented office space, hired a manager—a former student of mine—and began operations. The office had a marginally profitable existence, but our manager, I believe, was not as faithful to DHA as he should have been. This became apparent we won an airport contract with Volusia County, Georgia, just over the Florida state line. Just before the contract was signed, however, our Florida manager resigned. Subsequently we learned that the county had decided not to award the contract to DHA after all. Instead, it awarded the project to a newly created firm—a firm that happened to be owned by our former manager. We decided we had had enough. We completed our existing contracts and left Orlando.

Unlike in Orlando, DHA had a great run in Los Angeles.

We probably performed more final design contracts on its heavy rail system than any engineering consultant, including designing five underground stations and a mile and a half of double-barrel tunnel. In addition, we participated in the design of aerial structures for the Los Angeles Light Rail System and provided construction management services for bridge construction over the Los Angeles River. We were also involved in the design of major facilities at the Los Angeles International Airport, a new major police facility for the City of Los Angeles, and other structures of prominence in the Los Angeles area.

We became interested in practicing in the Los Angeles area when we were asked to be part of a team led by one of the largest and most highly respected engineering firms in the country. The team was being formed to pursue work on the proposed Los Angeles Heavy Rail System. We felt certain that the team would be selected to design a section so we agreed to join. Less than two months before submittals of qualifications for section designers were due, the prime consultant notified us that DHA had been eliminated from the team. By that time all the teams most likely to be selected had been formed. What do we do?

My two fellow firm principals, John M. Zimmer and R. Varadarajan, recommended that we form our own team. We did. We submitted our team's qualifications, got shortlisted, and made a presentation to the selection committee. Not only did we win, but we won the responsibility for designing the largest section to be let, which included two underground rail stations in downtown Los Angeles and the double-barrel rail tunnel. The firm that kicked us off its team? It got nothing.

Unfortunately, I never thought to express our deepest gratitude to the board of directors of the Southern California Rapid Transit District, now known as the Los Angeles County Metropolitan Transportation Authority, for the confidence it placed in our small minority-owned firm by giving us the largest contract under Phase I of its program. That took guts. I plan to correct my bad manners and properly thank the members of that board who gave us our big break in Los Angeles.

Shortly after DHA was selected and negotiated the contract to design the Civic Center and Fifth and Hill Street stations and the tunnel beginning at Union Station, we opened a Los Angeles office and began design work. I was in the Los Angeles office weekly, which made for a tough travel schedule from Washington. It only got tougher after I accepted an assignment to participate on a consulting board whose charge was to recommend how to restore the integrity of a tunnel whose breach had flooded downtown Chicago. I would begin my week in Washington, fly to Los Angeles, spend a day or two in the LA office, then take an overnight flight to Chicago. Upon arriving I would sleep for a few hours then spend the rest of the day participating in the board of consultants meeting. After our board completed its report with recommendations for action, I would take an evening flight back to Washington.

This routine continued for weeks until the crisis was over. This was a very challenging assignment and I was pleased to work with a great team of engineers, contractors, and government officials. Despite all the travel, it was worth it.

DHA's regional offices in Orlando, Los Angeles, and Chicago thrived while there was a lot of work in those cities, but we were not able to sustain them. It wasn't because we didn't have the engineering acumen; it was because we didn't have the business acumen—didn't have sufficiently strong office managers, I believe. As of this writing, our only satellite offices are in Silver Spring, Maryland, Atlanta, and Baltimore. Atlanta came on hard times due to the recession of the late 2000s, but I decided DHA would not retreat any further. We are growing and rebuilding that office again. I have also charged the DHA management team with leading DHA back to stable offices in Los Angeles and Chicago.

In the meantime, the projects we helped design, build, and manage all across the country are a source of pride wherever I go.

In Washington, there is the Capitol Visitors Center, where as part of the construction management team we oversaw the work of the contractors involved every step of the way in the $600 million, three-story center built fifty-five feet below the US Capitol. The project was the biggest addition in the history of the 200-year-old US Capitol—nearly three quarters of the size of the Capitol itself. I was privileged to represent my firm and its hard work at the center's grand opening in December 2008.

Not far from the Capitol, along the Anacostia River, is the 41,888-seat Nationals Park, home to the city's baseball team. The park is one of the prettiest in all of professional baseball, with 360-degree views of the entire metropolitan area. It was the nation's first Leadership in Energy and Environmental Design (LEED) accredited major league baseball stadium. DHA's unique design of the underdrain system for the playing field at Nationals Park was featured on the front page of the sports section of *USA Today.*

Along with our work on the baseball park in the nation's capital, we served as the structural and civil engineer for the Verizon Center, home to Washington's NBA franchise. We also provided civil and structural engineering and support for the 1.3-million-square-foot Gallery Place mixed use center adjacent to Verizon Center, which includes nine stories of residential space, office space, a movie theater, and 250,000 square feet of retail space, all connected to the Gallery Place Chinatown metro transit station. Designing the $350 million Gallery Place development was a particular challenge because of its constrained site in the middle of downtown Washington, atop and adjacent to one of the busiest stations in the Washington Metro system. Gallery Place also sits about a block from DHA's headquarters, so I get to see it from my office window each working day.

One of our biggest and longest-running projects is with the Metropolitan Washington Airports Authority as part of its $7 billion-plus program to upgrade and renovate the region's airports. For about twenty years we have participated in the management of just about every major construction project at Dulles International Airport and Ronald Reagan Washington National Airport, including building or renovating control towers, terminals, people mover stations, and runways and taxiways.

In 1989 I revisited one of my boyhood haunts in Chicago after we got a subcontract to provide civil and structural engineering design and construction observation services for the new Comiskey Park, across the street from the original Comiskey, where I used to watch the White Sox and Chicago Cardinals. It was a treat to be involved with a project like that, even though we left the project before completion of construction.

In Atlanta, we helped design and build the equestrian center at the Georgia International Horse Park for the 1996 Olympic Games, oversaw major improvements at Hartsfield-Jackson Atlanta International Airport, and have been assigned by the Federal Transit Administration to provide program management oversight for the innovative Atlanta Streetcar project that will connect the city's downtown hub with electric-powered transit. Atlanta also is home to one of the more unique projects DHA has ever been involved in: a 13,000-square-foot reptile complex and a 17,500-square-foot animal hospital at Zoo Atlanta.

In Los Angeles, we helped with design and construction management at Los Angeles International Airport and the civil engineering design for the city's new police facility. We also did civil engineering for a veteran's cemetery and provided construction management oversight services during the renovation of a bridge over the Los Angeles River that had to be carefully constructed in two phases to keep the trains running on time.

Projects often come with unique challenges.

In the 1990s we were involved in construction management for a $151 million expansion of the Baltimore Convention Center. But our work there extended beyond the convention center itself. In order to move forward with the expansion project, we had to strengthen and fortify a neighboring building, the Old Otterbein Church, which has been there since 1785.

Similarly, when we redesigned and oversaw remodeling of the hundred-year-old Shiloh Baptist Church in downtown Washington, we had to provide a new 33,000-square-foot building and an adjoining 1,500-seat auditorium while preserving three historic exterior brick walls. That feat was particularly tricky because the original church, amazingly enough, was built without a foundation. We won many accolades for our work at Shiloh Baptist, including awards from the Masonry Institute and the Washington Building Congress.

For all the signature projects we've been involved in, however, there have been hundreds and hundreds of other projects over the years that we worked on just as hard and cared about just as much.

For the past six plus years DHA has been providing civil engineering design and construction oversight professional services for the 1,570,000-square-foot City Center Project currently under construction in downtown Washington, DC, on the former DC Convention Center site. This mixed use project, being developed by Hines, encompasses 458 rental apartment units, 216 condominium units, 515,000 square feet of office space, and 1.5 acres of public plaza/park.

The second phase of the project is planned to include a 370-room luxury hotel, along with 110,000 additional square feet of retail space. This great contribution to downtown Washington, DC, will be welcomed with open arms when it becomes fully operational in mid-2014.

Our successes, I believe, were due in no small part to two driving principles that have guided me throughout the years and through the growth of DHA.

First, you have to take care of your clients.

Clients want and need to be involved in the process of a project every step of the way. If they're not, they will feel like they're not getting the value and attention they deserve. I expect my project managers to talk to their clients at least once a week, if not daily. My mentors taught me long ago that if we don't communicate well with our clients, we lose business and we get a bad reputation. At the end of a project we want the clients to be happy and we want to have lived up to their expectations—but if we don't communicate with the client every step of the way, we won't fully know their expectations, or what will make them happy when we're done.

It is always a pleasure to see a project go from design to concrete and steel, and the best part of any project is seeing it completed and in use. But to me, the gauge of whether we are successful on any project is whether the client is happy with the end product.

The other basic principle on which I built my business is based on the adage about slot machines: You've got to play to win.

From the day I started DHA, I've been fully committed. It's the first thing I think about when I rise in the morning, and usually the last thing I think about when I go to sleep at night. If you're going to be in the business, I believe, you've got to be in the business. You've got to be involved in all facets of your profession. That's part of the reason I have belonged to dozens of professional organizations, ranging from the American Council of Engineering Companies to the World Federation of Engineering Organizations. (I also happen to be a current or former member of other organizations that have even more colorful names, such as the Moles and the Beavers, two groups for professionals who are engaged in major design and/or heavy construction, and the Honorable Order of Kentucky Colonels.)

Most business is done through personal contact. If you don't put yourself in the position to have personal contact with potential clients, partners, and colleagues, you don't have a very good chance of getting their business. Being in the business—in every facet of the business—also puts you in contact with people who can change or influence your path forward. I could not have met the many mentors, partners, and associates I've been lucky enough to know if I was not fully engaged in the business and in the communities we serve.

Eight

The Other Side of Life

MY LIFE's emphasis has been on achieving the American Dream. Unfortunately my focus has been solely on the professional side of that dream. The other part—friends, family, marriage, children—I neglected.

I did not recognize this in sufficient time to correct the situation, and as a result I have paid a heavy price: three marriages, two divorces, and no children. Now that I'm in my later years, I find myself with a paucity of close personal relationships with family members and friends. The reason, I am sure, is my failure to maintain close ties with them because of my focus on business and building my professional life. The net result was predictable.

I have always wanted children. But instead of giving my time to trying to build a successful family, I focused my time and efforts on building DHA. As a result, I never found out if I could be the great father I believe I could have been. I also destroyed the dreams of some good people.

My best chance for a successful marriage with children was with Janet Jones Hampton. Jan was a great wife and I was a lousy husband. My focus was totally on the development of my new company and teaching career, not my new wife. Those early days together in Chicago, when I would spend so much of my time working while Jan was left to figure out life on her own in a city that was strange and new to her, were telling.

Our major cause of disagreement back then, and even before, had been when to have children. We discussed it often, and our differences were clear. She wanted to start a family immediately. I wanted to wait until we were more economically secure.

When we got married, Jan was studying for her doctorate at the University of Texas. I wanted her to get her degree before we got married. She did not want to wait, though, so I agreed that she should postpone completion of her studies in order for us to get married. In hindsight, that was a mistake. I now realize that I really was not ready for marriage at that time. Delaying marriage would have given me more time to become more stable in my career and to nurture my budding business plans, and it would have given Jan the time to finish her doctoral studies. In addition, delaying marriage a few years, I think, would have given us the financial and professional security that would have allowed us to start a family immediately after we were married, which is what Jan really wanted. If we would have tried to have children immediately regardless of our financial and professional situation, perhaps we would still be married today. We did not realize it at the time, but for both of us, it was our last opportunity for children. Hindsight, of course, is 20/20.

Instead of building a family together, I chose to build a business. It wasn't long before I realized I couldn't get enough time to devote to my business endeavors, and Jan realized I couldn't give her enough time to devote to building a family and the dreams she wanted to pursue. Eventually, I asked for my freedom. We sat at our kitchen table and agreed on a settlement, and I left. After waiting the required time, our uncontested divorce was approved by the District of Columbia. When my friend and mentor Jim Caywood learned I left Jan he said, "Delon, you are a fool." As far as achieving my goal of a family with children, Jim was right.

After we parted, Jan went on to get her doctorate from the Catholic University in Washington, DC.

Later she joined the faculty of George Washington University, from where she retired as associate professor emerita.

I have remained close to Jan and her family. Her father, Herman T. Jones, died prematurely. But her mother, Gwendolyn Jones, and I remained friends until her death in 2009 at the age of ninety-seven. Over the years I have visited Jan and her family in Doña Ana County, New Mexico. Considering the trauma I put Jan and her family through, I am honored that they still consider me a close family friend. She and her sister, Gayle Lewis, have provided substantial help to me in creating this book.

Jan and I remain good friends as well. I hope and believe she has forgiven me for destroying her—and my—dreams of family life and a happy marriage.

* * *

My second wife was Fay Myers Hampton, whom I met when she was an American Airlines flight attendant. We met on a flight from Washington, where she was based, to Chicago. I asked her to have dinner with me that night and she agreed. She was staying at the Sheraton Hotel on Chicago's North Side, where I picked her up. Her beauty overwhelmed me as I saw her walking across Michigan Avenue to my car. It was love at second sight. We went out and had a very pleasant dinner and good conversation. At the end of the evening, we exchanged contact information and promised to get together once we both returned to Washington. We did.

During our courtship we would often visit Fay's parents in Chicago. I really liked her parents. Her mother is a really sweet person. Her father was a fiery individual and very pro-union. I am not, so we would not let a meeting go by without a good-spirited debate about organized labor.

Fay and I got married at my home in Potomac, Maryland, a suburb of Washington. Only family and a few friends were present. My dear friend Rev. Jerry A. Moore Jr. performed the service. Due to work schedules, we postponed our honeymoon—a harbinger of the strain that work, once again, would put on our personal lives.

Unfortunately there was another strain on our marriage from the beginning. Prior to my meeting Fay, my mother and sister had moved from Benton Harbor, Michigan, to my home and had become part of my household. In hindsight, that was a mistake. As newlyweds, the constant presence of other people in our home while we were adjusting to each other presented a problem. Eventually, we decided that it would be better if my mother and sister moved out, and that it would be best if they returned to Chicago. That would let them be near the majority of their friends and remaining family and allow us to nurture our new marriage. The move was probably best for them, but for me it was a sad day when they left my home.

Along with the presence of my mother and sister, work life once again came between me and my new bride. Between my business travel schedule and Fay's work as a flight attendant, we did not have much time together. Here again, I devoted too much time to DHA and not enough time to my wife. It didn't help that I'm not the best at interpersonal communication. We had a hard time connecting—or even finding the time in our busy schedules to connect. Compounding this was Fay's decision to return to college. She enrolled at the University of Maryland to pursue a degree in sociology. So while I was trying to build a business, she was trying to build a new career. In between, we neglected to build a life together. Shortly after Fay earned her sociology degree, she told me she wanted to pursue a master's degree at Purdue University. She also told me she wanted a divorce.

Once again, I found myself sitting at the kitchen table across from another soon-to-be ex-wife, working out a financial settlement. I helped Fay pack her car, and then she was gone. As it turned out, she did not like the curriculum at Purdue University. The fact that she was working as a graduate student assistant under the supervision of one of my former classmates, then a member of Purdue's faculty, may also have been a factor in her decision to leave Purdue and finish her academic studies at the University of Illinois. In essence, I later realized, she followed my academic footsteps in reverse. She also, like me, would be married three times. According to her sister Ava, the third time was the charm.

Ava and I remained close friends. On one of my visits to Chicago, she set up a dinner between Fay and me. We had a friendly dinner but I guess the damage to our relationship was too great. That was the last time I saw Fay. She was kind enough, however, to provide me a copy of a picture of the two of us taken the day of our wedding for my book, for which I am grateful.

* * *

Sonia Milagros Hampton and I met by accident. I was having lunch at a hotel close to my office; she was having lunch with a woman I knew. They stopped by my table and I was introduced to Sonia. Later that day, I called our mutual friend and got Sonia's telephone number. I called her and we began to date, and eventually we got married.

Shortly after we were married, I found myself in a situation similar to the one I had inserted Fay into.

Sonia asked if she could bring her mother, Teresa Milagros, to live with us. I said yes. After her mother had
been with us for a while, Sonia asked if her nephew
could come to live with us. She wanted to give him the
opportunity for a better education. Again I said yes.

Fortunately, our personal and professional situa-
tions are different than when I was with Fay or with
Jan. My business is on solid ground, my finances are
secure, and my life is more mature. Sonia and I have
learned to adjust to each other, and it looks like we will
be together until death do us part. At the same time,
I have learned a lot about being a husband—from Sonia and from others. Sonia believes that when I was
growing up I never learned how to "give." She is probably right. I was raised in a loving family, as far as the
women in my life were concerned. But when it came
to adult males in my life, I received little of value. I
didn't meet my natural father until I was nearly grown.
Even then, my only relationship with him was limited to a few short days in which he virtually ignored
me. The father who raised me, Uless Hampton, had
almost no relationship with me during my formative
years. And the man who replaced him as my mother's second husband, David Mixon, was an alcoholic
for whom I had no respect. In a nutshell, I never had
an environment from which I could learn how to be

a good husband or a good father. That hurt me later when I became a husband.

But it isn't just my lack of good male role models growing up that kept me from having better relationships with my spouses. One of my worst faults is that I have not been very good at personal communications. I tend to keep my feelings to myself. When I have problems, I tend to address them alone. That characteristic probably came from the fact that while growing up I rarely had a serious conversation about anything of substance with an adult member of my family. As wonderful and as caring as my mother was, I had to make all of the major decisions of my early life on my own, without input from her or others. As long as my decisions and actions were legal, had no adverse impact on anyone, and produced a positive result, I was allowed to move forward. Even as I grew older, I typically made my life's decisions without consulting anyone, or without fully considering what the effect of those decisions might have on others or even on me. That sort of decision making works when you're a single young man getting through college or pursuing a profession or building a business. It doesn't work very well when you have a partner in life and are trying to build a lasting relationship or family.

NINE

Engineering Life

IN CONTRAST to my personal life, my professional life has been exemplary.

My career in academics and my career in the practice of engineering have both been unqualified successes that give me much reason to be thankful and grateful for those who helped me along my way. As a product of inner-city Chicago whose parents never made it to high school, the odds of my succeeding in academics probably weren't too great. But in the pursuit of a better life, I was always determined to go to college. I just knew that if I wanted to be successful, I needed a good education. As a result I earned a bachelor's degree from the University of Illinois as well as master's and PhD degrees from Purdue University. Both schools are among the best engineering colleges in the nation. Later, as an educator, I taught some of the brightest engineering students in the nation, and published papers in professional and technical publications. In addition, I have received honorary doctorates from Purdue and the New Jersey Institute of Technology, and have received other honors from the University of Illinois and elsewhere. I have given the commencement address to graduating engineering students at the University of Maryland and at San José State University.

I also have served as president of the American Society of Civil Engineers; served on the governing council of the National Academy of Engineering, our nation's premier honorific engineering society; was elected to membership in the American Academy of Arts and Sciences, our nation's second-most prestigious honorific society for engineers; and served as chair of the business member board of governors of the American Public Transportation Association (APTA), as well as two terms on APTA's executive committee and three terms on its board of direction.

As a result of my contributions to my profession and my successes, I have also been honored by being appointed to leadership roles in a wide variety of other national organizations, including the board of overseers of the Malcolm Baldrige National Quality Award; the National Building Museum's board of directors; and as a board member and treasurer of the Center for National Policy.

Throughout my life I have tried to give back to my profession. I've also tried to give back to my nation, through my service in the US Army and in the US Naval Reserve.

Only in America could I have had such a journey. I know this. And I am forever grateful to my country, to my profession, to my family and my friends for helping me along the way.

No organization is more prestigious in the field of engineering than the American Society of Civil Engineers. Founded in 1852 when twelve of the early engineers of modern America met at the Croton Aqueduct in New York State to not only celebrate an engineering feat but also to set a foundation for the future of the profession, ASCE today represents more than 140,000 engineers worldwide and is the oldest national engineering society in the United States. It is the premiere organization to advance professional knowledge and improve the practice of engineering with the understanding that, ultimately, what we do as engineers affects everyone in society.

American Society of Civil Engineers

Shortly after arriving in Washington, DC, I became active in ASCE's National Capital Section. I began attending its meetings and became an active member of its committees. These activities led to positions as committee chair, section officer, and eventually section president. In addition to building a network of colleagues—something that's important for anyone in any business—my involvement in ASCE and other organizations helped hone my leadership skills. That proved helpful in building a business and beyond.

ASCE's Geotechnical Engineering Division has always been closest to my heart. I love those "Geos." As far back as 1964, the Division appointed me as its Secretary to the International Society of Soil Mechanics and Foundation Engineering. I represented ASCE at the international society's executive committee meetings and had the opportunity to sit at the feet and learn from some of the world's greatest geotechnical engineers.

In 1998, after working my way through the organizational hierarchy, I decided to seek the position of national president of ASCE. Never before had the group had a black president, and I was determined to become its first. I felt I had the proper academic and the professional credentials by then, and I thought I could make a difference by making the organization stronger and better. My friends and colleagues at ASCE's National Capital Section, as well as others across the country, supported me throughout my campaign. In addition, I was fortunate enough to enlist the support of my good friend C. R. "Chuck" Penonni, ASCE's past president, to lead my campaign, advocate on my behalf, and give the nominating speech in my support. Chuck did a great job and was a key to my success, along with my fellow National Capital Section members and my many supporters within ASCE.

In October 1999 I became president of ASCE—the first and only black president of a major national American engineering society. I had come a long way from the South Side of Chicago and my years of trying to break the color barrier and find an entry-level job in engineering. Unfortunately I would soon learn that ASCE, as other groups—and my profession as a whole—still had a long way to go toward improving equality in the field of engineering.

I also learned quickly that being president of the American Society of Civil Engineers entails a lot of international work outside of America that can be both exhausting and enlightening.

Shortly after I assumed office as ASCE's president, I received a visit from a delegation headed by the then president-elect of the Institution of Civil Engineers (ICE) of the United Kingdom. He wanted to ascertain our interest in joining with that organization to create a worldwide civil engineering organization headed by ASCE and

ICE. After much discussion, the two associations created a joint study group to come up with a framework for such an organization. Creating a worldwide civil engineering society would have been a huge leap for ASCE. It could have dramatically changed the engineering profession, and possibly made it easier for engineers to work anywhere around the world. But despite the tremendous effort put forth by working groups from both organization, and the sound logic behind the creation of the proposed international group, agreement could not be reached by the two governing bodies to proceed.

While negotiations between ASCE and ICE were occurring, the president-elect of the ICE invited and ASCE's executive director and me to his inauguration and I accepted. The festivities began the night before with a black tie reception, followed by dinner at the ICE headquarters. At dinner, the table was set for a hundred people. Seating was assigned so that guests did not sit beside the person they came with. The next morning the incoming president was installed and gave his inaugural address. While he was giving his speech, his name was being chiseled into one of the building's first floor columns, as is the group's custom. It was a very unique experience for me.

After the United Kingdom, I went to Panama to represent ASCE at the ceremony transferring ownership of the Panama Canal from the United States to Panama. There, I stood alongside others at one of the great engineering marvels of our time. ASCE considers it one of the seven wonders of the modern world, along with other great structures such as the Channel Tunnel, the Empire State Building, the Golden Gate Bridge, and the Zuiderzee Works in the Netherlands. The weather was lousy, but no one minded the rain. Happiness reigned supreme. Irv Mendenhall, ASCE's past president, and his lovely wife, Sally, joined me as part of the official ASCE delegation.

It was common for spouses to travel on ASCE delegations abroad, which made the trips even more enjoyable. Even before I became president of the group, Sonia and I traveled with previous ASCE president Jim Poirot and his lovely wife, Raeda, as part of an ASCE delegation to Chile and Argentina. Jim has left us and I am deeply saddened by his passing. He was a great engineer, an outstanding engineering manager, and a very dear and supportive friend.

Being a leader of a major professional organization also occasionally put me in some prestigious company. During the visit to Chile, for instance, we had an audience with Chilean President Eduardo Frei Ruiz-Tagle. Toward the end of my tenure, I had the honor of leading an ASCE delegation in a ceremony to Plains,

Georgia, where we conveyed our organization's Hoover Medal for distinguished public service to former US President Jimmy Carter. I unfortunately never got the opportunity to meet South African President Nelson Mandela, but I did tour the prison on Robben Island where he was once held.

In India and China, Sonia and I led ASCE delegations on learning and relationship building. The travel distances were great, but the hospitality was outstanding and we had wonderful exchanges of ideas. Due to the shortness of available time in countries there was little opportunity for sightseeing. However, we did manage to see some of the greatest engineering feats in that part of the world, including the Forbidden City and the Great Wall in China and the Taj Mahal in India. The trips were excellent from both professional and technical aspects and were wonderful opportunities for the sharing of knowledge and the making of new friends.

In other parts of the world I saw engineering from another perspective. In Turkey, for instance, I was part of an ASCE delegation that toured areas that had been recently devastated by a major earthquake. With our counterparts from Turkey and other parts of the world, we exchanged ideas on earthquake engineering design and construction.

Sonia and I also led an ASCE delegation to South Africa. Our first stop was in Cape Town following a seventeen-hour nonstop flight from Atlanta. From Cape Town we drove to Johannesburg, stopping on the way to spend a day touring a major aluminum plant. While in Johannesburg, we met with the South African Institution of Civil Engineering (then known as the South African Society of Civil Engineers) to discuss issues of mutual concern and visited the capital, Pretoria. We also went to the town of Soweto, where we toured an elementary school. The students were bright and energetic and I had the opportunity to speak to them, which I greatly enjoyed. The sad part of the visit was the poor physical condition of the school. In one of the classrooms I visited there was a large hole in the roof. I was impressed by the energy and enthusiasm of the students and their apparent belief that they could do well despite the hardships they faced. On the other end of the social spectrum, we also had a chance to visit my former brother-in-law, the Honorable Delano Lewis, who at the time was the US ambassador to South Africa. Sonia and I also had the pleasure of having pre-dinner drinks with him and his lovely wife, Gayle.

While in Africa, Sonia and I also took a weekend in Zimbabwe. We had visited game preserves in

South Africa but did not see all of the big five game members: the lion, elephant, Cape buffalo, leopard, and rhinoceros. Those animals we had not seen in South Africa we saw in Zimbabwe. I will always remember sitting on the side of the road one quiet evening and watching a massive herd of elephants return from the nearby river on their way to their nightly resting spot.

I had heard about the mighty Zambezi River and decided to take a rafting trip down it. The starting point for the trip was just below Victoria Falls. The morning of the trip I said goodbye to Sonia and boarded a raft with six other people plus the guide. The morning segment was fun but uneventful. We stopped for lunch, after which all the other people on the raft boarded buses to return to their hotels. Only the guide and I were left to negotiate the afternoon leg of the trip. We boarded the raft and headed for the first rapid, which was named "Mother." Immediately upon entering the rapid, a large wave hit the front of the raft. It soared into the air, turned over, and I wound up under it. I had forgotten what we were told to do under such a circumstance so I simply floated through the remainder on my back. When I got to the end one of the guides escorting us in kayaks told me to get out of the water due to the threat of alligators. Such an

attack was possible but not probable since the alligators would have to come over Victoria Falls and the
drop would most likely kill them. Fortunately I never
found out whether or not an alligator could make it
over the falls.

Following the weekend in Zimbabwe, we returned
to South Africa to complete our business. The last major event was a dinner given in our honor by the South
African Institution of Civil Engineering. At the time
a dear friend, former DHA employee and former fellow faculty member at Howard University, Dr. Lilia
Abron Robinson, who operates a company in South
Africa, accepted my invitation to join us, and it was
great to have her. The trip to South Africa was a most
professionally and socially rewarding experience that
I shall never forget.

Back in the United States, I worked on several major initiatives while I was president of ASCE. One of
the most fulfilling was the creation of the group's Outstanding Projects and Leaders (OPAL) Awards. The
awards are given each year to people for outstanding
lifetime contributions to the engineering profession and
to a project which embodies the essence of engineering ingenuity in design and construction. The awards
are presented during an impressive ceremony. Giving
recognition where it is due is great, but ASCE must

continue to ensure the quality of each future awardee. It is better to have no winner than one our profession recognizes as unqualified. When Gregs Thomopulos, PE, won the OPAL award for management, I was especially proud. Gregs is one of only two black engineers I know of who has become CEO of a major engineering or construction firm. During my term as ASCE president, another issue I pushed was honoring our heroes. My colleagues in the Geotechnical Division picked up the mantle after I left, and to this date ASCE annually honors geotechnical engineering heroes for outstanding contributions to our profession and society as a whole.

As I faced the end of my term as ASCE president, I began thinking about what I might say in my valedictory address. I decided that I would take a page from ASCE itself. One of the group's signature events is the release of its annual Report Card for America's Infrastructure, which rates the state of our nation's bridges, highways, and water systems. The Report Card is always a highlight of the year for ASCE and garners lots of attention. I decided that I would do a report card on ASCE. My hope was that it might lead to future improvements in the society. Remember from my academic years, I was considered a tough grader. My ASCE report card can be summarized as follows:

Topic	Grade	Critique
Masters as the first professional degree	D	Great idea, lousy execution
Continuing education requirements for ASCE membership	F	No guts, no glory
Image and stature of engineers	D+	Lots of talk, little substance
Diversity	D	Little interest, little effort
Internationalization	A	Solid vision coupled with great effort
Public policy	D	Much action, little value
ASCE institutes	B	Good approach, right direction, sincerity of effort

Surprisingly, my valedictory speech received a standing ovation. Sonia joined me onstage to receive her Past First Lady's Pin and to accept congratulatory applause for her contributions to ASCE.

American Council of Engineering Companies

Shortly after creating DHA, I joined and became active in the Metropolitan Washington chapter of another organization, then known as the American Consulting Engineers Council (ACEC), now known as the American Council of Engineering Companies. ACEC/Metrpolitan Washington Chapter consisted of a great group of guys who worked hard in support of the organization and enjoyed each other's companionship both in work and in play. John Bachner, a great guy and friend, was its executive director. Over the years I worked hard within ACEC/Metropolitan Washington Chapter and eventually was elected its president. Later on, through continued effort and dedication to ACEC, I was elected to its national governing body.

During the latter part of my tenure as president of ACEC/Metropolitan Washington Chapter, we hosted the national organization's annual meeting. One of my favorite buildings, the National Building Museum, was selected as the venue for the convention banquet. It's not surprising that an engineer would be impressed by a building dedicated to telling the stories of architecture, engineering, and design, but if you ever get a chance to see the National Building Museum, you should. A 1,200-foot-long terra-cotta frieze depicting Civil War troops runs the length of the building, and its 75-foot-tall Corinthian columns are some of the tallest in the world. The exterior of the building, modeled after Rome's Palazzo Farnese, makes it unique among the typical government-style buildings in the District of Columbia. And when you walk in and see the 234 busts that represent each of the building trades—masons, carpenters, architects, engineers, and many others—you get a sense of what it takes to build such a building. Designed and built by US Army Gen. Montgomery Meigs and civil engineers between 1882 and 1887, the building was originally meant to process pension payments to Civil War veterans, but today is used for purposes more befitting of its grandeur, such as presidential inaugural balls. I came to know the National Building Museum's then president, Susan Henshaw-Jones, and was eventually invited to join the museum's board of directors.

My involvement in ACEC was outwardly cordial, but it was evident that some of that group did not appreciate my presence. One glaring example occurred while I was the group's vice president of international affairs. One afternoon I was in my office and received a call from the president of the Canadian Consulting Engineers Council, who invited me to dinner. I asked why he was in town, and he informed me it was for a meeting with the president and vice president of ACEC/America. You would think my fellow ACEC members would let the chairman of international affairs know about such a meeting, but no one ever told me anything about this. If my friend had not called to invite me to dinner, I probably would not have known about the meeting, even though I had the responsibility for international activities for the society. To me it felt like a sad example of disrespect, and I hope it did not also reflect discrimination.

While the chair of ACEC/Canada and I were meeting in my office prior to departing for dinner, the ACEC/America chair and vice chair stopped by my office, for what purpose I do not know. That experience left serious certainty in my mind of the lack of respect of the then volunteer hierarchy of national ACEC to diversity. Nevertheless, hope springs eternal, so toward the end of my tenure on the executive committee I vied for the position of ACEC chairman and president, but it came as no surprise that my quest was unsuccessful. I decided I had no future in the organization, so I did not renew our firm's membership and left the group.

National Academy of Engineers

One day in 1992, while opening my office mail, I received a great surprise. I had been elected to membership in the National Academy of Engineering (NAE). The Academy is considered the pinnacle of the engineering profession, and its American and foreign members are considered to be among the world's most accomplished engineers. To become a member, one must be elected by his or her peers. When I opened my mail and learned I had been elected, I was thrilled, but shocked. I did not know I had been nominated. Later, following years of inquiry, I learned that a dear friend had nominated me. According to the official election citation, I was nominated "for outstanding contributions to education and practice in geotechnical and transportation engineering, and for leadership in engineering education for minorities." Years later, I was elected to serve on NAE's governing council.

In addition to my tenure on the NAE's executive council, I had other interesting and challenging assignments during my engineering life. One was as a member of the National Research Council committee that studied the cost escalation which occurred on the "Big Dig" tunnel project in Boston. It was an interesting and challenging assignment. A big surprise to me was that when that job began the federal government did not permit cost estimates for federally funded projects to include annual price escalation due to inflation in project budgets. Therefore, nearly every federal construction project at that time was guaranteed to produce a cost overrun unless the costs of labor and materials decreased or cost estimates buried such costs in their labor and material costs.

A second was a committee assignment to evaluate the US Army Corps of Engineers' plan for development of the Upper Mississippi River. Some citizens and municipalities in that area had serious concerns about the possible negative impact of the proposed development on their region. Our teams submitted their reports and they were accepted and published by the funding agency, the National Research Council.

Another study in which I participated dealt with the evaluation of the soil dynamics research being done by the US Army Corps of Engineers Waterways Experiment Station, the research facility in Vicksburg, Mississippi, that was created after the Great Mississippi Flood of 1927 to find better ways to prevent floods and other disasters. It was an interesting assignment which also provided me with the opportunity to visit with one of my former Howard University students, then working at the Waterways Experiment Station.

One of the most heartrending assignments I've ever had was my work on a National Research Council committee created to study the causes of the devastation to the levees around the city of New Orleans as a result of Hurricane Katrina. When the hurricane washed ashore in August 2005, the storm surge caused more than fifty failures of levees and flood walls that were designed to protect the city and its suburbs. As a result of these failures, an estimated 100,000 homes and businesses throughout 80 percent of New Orleans were flooded.

We had all seen on television the damage that resulted. But when our team made its first inspection of the damaged areas, the first thing I realized was that the devastation appeared to be much worse when viewed on the ground and in person. Furthermore, seeing the terrible losses and physical conditions to which the people of New Orleans were subjected was tragic. The storm killed more than 1,800 people, but it also left tens of thousands more struggling to survive in the Louisiana summer heat without proper food, water, sanitation, or shelter.

Along with my committee's study, there were numerous other investigations into the levee failures in New Orleans. They all agreed on the basic causes: poor design, poor maintenance, and poor preparation. In my view, there is no doubt that much of the devastation from Hurricane Katrina could have been prevented if the United States had been willing to pay the price for adequate protection.

TEN

Engineering Equality

I THINK it's safe to say that over the years and through
my involvement in all facets of my chosen career, I've
come to know the engineering profession pretty well.

But after more than a half-century in the business—and a half-century after the Civil Rights Act of
1964—I know of only two black engineers who have
become CEOs of major engineering or construction
companies.

There's something wrong with that picture.

Addressing equality in engineering requires addressing a vast panoply of hurdles that every minority
man or woman must face along every step of the way
if he or she wants to become successful in my—and
other—industries.

All across America, many talented minority engineers are too often shunted to positions in business

development or other areas instead of into C-track positions that can lead to the CEO's office. Why? Because due to the presence of black leadership in major cities in the United States, having a minority engineer in business development can help land business for a firm. But shame on these talented minority engineers for accepting a position in sales or business development if their true interest is in the practice of engineering. Shame on upper management as well if they push talented minority engineers into positions where their talents aren't fully utilized, just because they need more minority faces in the business development department. Such actions denigrate the efforts of all those minority engineers who toiled tirelessly to the benefit of their firms, our nation, and the engineering profession. There are cadres of unsung heroes who served their country and profession well with little recognition from their companies or their peers.

Because young minorities don't see people who look like them in leadership positions in major engineering and construction firms, they are less likely to choose engineering as a career. People who can conquer engineering have the capacity to become successful in any profession, because engineers are taught to think logically. So why should they choose engineering where their path to the top is paved with so many hurdles and so few examples of success?

The only way to attract minorities into engineering in significant numbers is to show them that if they work hard and play by the rules, every position, right up to chief executive office, is open to them when they demonstrate they have the skills. Unfortunately, our profession's leaders have not been willing to accept the challenge and remove the barriers. Our engineering leaders keep doing the same things over and over expecting different results. That's one of the definitions of insanity.

I once gave a speech to the business members of the American Public Transit Association. I told them that if I had children, I could not in good conscience encourage them to enter the engineering profession. Even though the 1964 Civil Rights Act was supposed to foster equality all across our society, there is a great paucity of people who look like me at the top of engineering and construction firms. As with other professions, engineering and construction businesses spend a lot of time, money, and effort to abide by the "letter of the law" regarding the Civil Rights Act. But that doesn't necessarily mean they abide by the spirit of the law and its intended purposes. I wouldn't want a child of mine to face the hurdles and lack of top opportunities that they would face in the engineering profession as a minority. Of course if I had a child who, despite my views on the engineering profession, decided to choose it for a career, I would give him or her my strongest support. But I wouldn't encourage my children to follow in my footsteps.

Engineering societies and minorities

I thought I might be able to change some of this when I became the first—and so far only—black president of the American Society of Civil Engineers. I was a bit naïve. ASCE had a black executive director and projected a positive image of race relations. However, I began to figure out that not all was as it seemed. In 1999, right after I became the president-elect and a member of ASCE's executive committee, various personnel issues came to light during my time as president-elect and then president that to me felt rooted in racism, especially some problems involving the then executive director and the committee devoted to issues related to minorities and women.

At one stage I also filed ethics charges against two of ASCE's senior staff members who, I perceived, colluded with an ASCE leader to deny the full participation of the ASCE Committee on Minorities and Women in Civil Engineering in all of the affairs and opportunities that ASCE presents. (This committee is now known as the ASCE Committee on Diversity and Women in Civil Engineering, which implies that women's issues fall outside the realm of diversity issues, an idea with which I believe few people would concur.) Usually such charges are adjudicated promptly by the ASCE Ethics Committee and its decision forwarded to the ASCE Executive Committee for action, if deemed appropriate. Yet years after I made these ethics charges, I still have not heard of anything being done about it. To me, this simply shows a lack of respect to me as a past president and honorary member, and to all minority and female members of ASCE.

Concurrently, a case of sexual harassment was reported against a white ASCE leader by a black female staff member. Rather than press charges, the reported victim left the organization and no action was taken against the accused.

ASCE's current executive director is a strong supporter of affirmative action. Unfortunately, even with his strong support, the organization still does not have a grip on the matter. While other organizations are strengthening their support of affirmative action, ASCE appears to be taking a step backward, in my opinion. Most organizations seriously dedicated to equality and affirmative action make those issues a high priority, but

ASCE at its 2012 board meeting actually reduced the role and the importance of its committee dedicated to this issue.

Throughout my tenure in ASCE's leadership, I was very disappointed by the discrimination I perceived on the part of a very few staffers and elected officers. That said, I did receive strong support from the great preponderance of the membership and staff. For that I shall be eternally grateful. We had our disagreements. But for the most part whenever I met with ASCE members, I was treated with respect, kindness, and friendship.

I want to express my deep appreciation to all those ASCE staff members and volunteers who served me and ASCE with distinction before, during, and after my tenure as ASCE president, as well as all the members of ASCE who, even when they disagreed with me, gave me and our society their support and respect.

When I completed my passage through the presidents' chairs at ASCE—president-elect, president, and past president—I maintained my membership in the society, but I did not remain active in its affairs. There were just too many bad memories for me there. However, I have now resumed attending meetings, conferences, and past presidents' events again because I have a lot of very dear friends who are members with whom

I would have very little contact outside of ASCE. I've also decided that I might be able to help broaden ASCE's commitment to diversity at such events. I attended the 2012 ASCE Annual Conference in Memphis and had a wonderful time with fellow past presidents and friends. I also joined my fellow geotechnical engineers at the 2012 Terzaghi Lecture and dinner held in Oakland, California, a highlight event each year to which I am most pleased to have been invited.

Unfortunately, I also experienced how hard it is to drive change and equality in the engineering profession at the other major engineering society I've long been involved in, the National Academy of Engineering.

Shortly after I became an NAE member, the sitting president, Dr. William Wolf, and the group's council launched an effort to get minorities and women into and involved in the engineering profession. This effort went on for years without much visible success. Eventually it went the way of the dodo bird. I think it went that way due to the lack of vision and interest by those charged with administering the program. Another cause was the co-opting of the program by those whose sole interest was limited to supporting women in engineering. Also contributing to the demise of this program was the apparent unwillingness of NAE to attack the problem at its wellhead, at the leadership of private and public sector engineering and construction organizations. These are the people who can have the greatest impact on attracting minority engineers into the engineering profession by the way they hire, manage, and provide minorities with equal opportunities for learning, promotion, and success.

Both ASCE and NAE have professed a desire for including more minorities in their programs, and having minorities involved in their organizations. But in my opinion, neither has been successful to any significant degree. The main reason for this, I believe, is a lack of commitment. I think they fear adverse reaction from their majority membership.

Federal contracting and minorities

Shortly after DHA was created, the federal government started the DBE (Disadvantaged Business Enterprise) and the WBE (Women's Business Enterprise) programs to try to ensure that at least 10 percent of highway, transit, and airport contracts went to women and minority businesses. Such programs were needed and long overdue to address the hostile environment for minorities and women in the engineering and construction industry.

When the minority program started, it was excellent. Successful participation required firms to be well-managed, effective in business development, and technically capable. Then unfortunately Congress, in its infinite wisdom, turned the program into a political football and welfare system, twisting it into one that protects big businesses more than small businesses—much to the detriment of the program and its participants. At one time, if a business owner wanted to participate in the program, he or she had to learn all aspects of good management. That helped create not just equal opportunities for minority contractors, but also strong and economically viable companies. Today, though, all that's required to participate in the program is to have an income level below some arbitrarily defined government cap. In doing so, our federal government has inhibited the success of the program by arbitrarily requiring low personal and business financial caps to participate in the DBE program, probably in response to lobbying by large firms. The goal of the program should be to have more women and minority participation in business at all levels and to provide them the opportunity to develop to their maximum potential. The low cap on personal wealth and business income that's required for participation makes it difficult for business owners who are just starting out to keep their firm financially afloat and still qualify for the programs. It also may foster fraud and abuse, because business owners may be reluctant to provide a full disclosure of their financial resources just so they can qualify for the program. As a result, the growth of minority- and women-owned businesses has been stunted by the program, not helped.

Minority, DBE, and WBE firms are further disadvantaged by federal, state, and local governmental agencies because most of these agencies don't adequately monitor and police the role of prime consultants on government contracts. Some prime contractors claim they cannot fulfill their commitments or clients' requirements because they cannot find qualified eligible firms with which to subcontract. I would be willing to bet that is seldom, if ever, the case. My experience and belief is that the goals are too often purposely not met in order to increase the profitability of the firm required to meet the DBE, WBE, and minority goals. Furthermore, very seldom, if ever, have I seen a prime consultant penalized for not fulfilling a DBE, WBE, or minority business goal. In my forty years in business, only once has a government owner of a project on which DHA has been involved asked our prime consultant to account for his or her lack of commitment to fulfilling MBE/WBE and/or minority subcontractor goals and threatened possible punitive action if he or she did not meet the commitment. That occurred in 2011. In general, enforcement of the goals at all levels of government appears to be lax. Our firm has been subject to unfulfilled contractual financial commitments by prime consultants with no repercussions to the prime consultants failing to meet their stated commitments. Shortly before this writing, DHA appears to have experienced just such a case of injustice by a prime consultant. This apparent injustice, if I am correct, should be obvious to the agency, but to my knowledge nothing has been done to investigate it.

Engineering and construction still lags behind other segments of our society in assuring equal opportunities. Federal and state governments need to take their oversight responsibilities more seriously to ensure a level playing field for all, including ensuring that prime consultants fully comply with their contractual commitments to their minority, small, women, and disadvantaged business enterprise subcontractors. Why have the programs at all, if their rules aren't enforced?

Start from the beginning to address equality

My good friends Elijah B. Rogers and Dr. Donald H. Smith, and my niece, Stacy L. Douglas, Esq., will probably be chagrined by what I am about to write. But it is something I feel very strongly about.

Minorities and women have to begin to accept partial responsibility for the failure of many of their members to achieve the American Dream. They have been and are still being subjected to de facto discrimination and, thus, deprived of access to equal opportunity. But remember the saying: "The good Lord helps those who help themselves." Young minorities and women must take more initiative and responsibility in demanding equal opportunity, rights, and access to the American Dream, as well as preparing themselves to achieve it. They must not passively accept discriminatory practices nor take being cheated in silence.

My generation grew up during a time of de jure segregation. Freedom from the shackles of de jure segregation was the result of pressure put on our federal government by the civil rights movement, led by the late Dr. Martin Luther King Jr., in which blacks, along with white friends and other supporters, protested, rallied for, and demanded the full rights of citizenship. They all believed in the principles upon which the United States professed to have been founded—the right to freedom, liberty, and the pursuit of happiness. Our nation was also fortunate during that critical time that Lyndon Baines Johnson, a Southerner, was president. I do not believe that any of his predecessors nor contemporaries would have had the political will, political skill, and respect from our Congress to crown the sacrifices of Dr. King, and the civil rights movement, with passage of the Civil Rights Act of 1964. Our nation—and particularly its black community—does not give President Johnson proper accolades for getting that controversial bill through Congress. I have never heard his name mentioned during Black History Week. What a shame. Without President Johnson's leadership, stature, and political acumen, the 1964 Civil Rights Act would have been much later arriving. It is sad that we have essentially ignored the critical role he played in ridding our nation of de jure segregation.

Leadership matters.

I recall one day receiving a call from Kansas State University's emeritus professor, Charles H. Scholer, the father of one of my fellow graduate students in the civil engineering program at Purdue University and, subsequently, a member of its faculty. He invited me to join him for breakfast the next day, and I accepted. The morning before I departed home for my meeting with Professor Scholer, I glanced at the *Washington Post*. One of its major stories was that then president John F. Kennedy had withdrawn his application for membership in the Cosmos Club because it had turned down Carl Rowan's application for membership. Rowan was a prominent African-American journalist. The Cosmos Club, at the time, was thought by many to be Washington's most prestigious private club. It was intimated that the real reason President Kennedy withdrew his application was the probability that his application, then under consideration, would also be turned down and he wanted to avoid that embarrassment. At that time it was believed by many that the Cosmos Club had difficulty voting politicians into membership. I met Professor Scholer at the Cosmos Club and we had an enjoyable breakfast, without incident—although our black waiter did seem a bit uncomfortable.

When one reads big city newspapers or watches TV news, one can see the other side of the story of minorities in America—young minority group members maiming and killing each other and going to prison for it. I recall reading Willard Motley's book *Knock on Any Door* about a young Italian-American boy whose motto was "Live fast, die young, and have a good-looking corpse." Unfortunately, there appears to be too big of a percentage of minority youth who have adopted that philosophy. I have no sympathy for them when our legal system calls them to account for their crimes. There are plenty of opportunities for health, happiness, and success in life if one is willing to study hard and to work for it. As for those not willing to pay the price for success and who choose the route of criminality: I empathize with them, but I have no sympathy for them. They will have chosen a route that will lead them to prison and/or death while causing great pain to those whom they harm and their families and friends.

Late in 2010 I happened to be watching CNN and saw a segment on young blacks killing each other in the city of Chicago. The segment showed a CNN reporter accompanying a young black high school student on his walk from home school. The conversation was about the dangers to high school students, such as being murdered on the way to and from school. All of a sudden I realized that the kid on the CNN segment was a student at the high school I transferred to in order to improve the quality of the education I was receiving. When I attended Englewood High School, it was located in a safe neighborhood with no threats to students. I had transferred there, in fact, because the school I was supposed to go to was a worse school and in a neighborhood—the one in which I lived—that had more than its share of gangs and violence. It was too bad to see that Englewood High School and the neighborhoods surrounding it were now subject to the same kinds of dangers and idiocy of gangs as well.

Thomas Sowell, while a professor at Stanford University, wrote a book in which he traced the economic progress of various ethnic groups from the time they reached the shores of America to the time that he wrote the book. He found that the then two most prosperous ethnic groups were the Jewish and Japanese peoples. On average, he found, they generally limited themselves to two children per family and provided their children the opportunity to be educated at our nation's most prestigious universities. This makes good sense. They also believed in the "spare the rod, spoil the child" concept—a concept that I support.

Sowell's book shows that the way for low-income families to steer their way out of poverty is to limit family size and ensure that their children receive a good education. I believe that states the obvious. Therefore, I cannot sympathize with poor families who have more children than they can afford and as a result must hold out their hands for welfare. Nor can I understand religions that encourage poor families to have more children than they can afford in order to increase the size of their flocks and further enrich their coffers. When I was growing up, families who were on welfare tried to hide it from their neighbors. Welfare was a badge of shame. Today, many people on welfare seem to flaunt it. Is our present welfare system causing more harm than good? I do not believe that question has been satisfactorily answered.

One definition of insanity, as I've suggested earlier, is repeatedly doing the same thing and expecting different results. I think we are doing that when it comes to many issues involving minorities in America.

You cannot blame the present conditions solely on racism and/or poverty. That would just be making an excuse for doing nothing.

All of my college friends came from poor, working class families and achieved much success in their chosen professions as physicians, teachers, dentists, lawyers, educators, engineers, architects, scientists, social workers, government officials, university professors, business leaders, architects, and so forth. We were part of a most productive generation, the Greatest Generation, and have passed the baton to our children who are also on the road to success.

Unfortunately today, there are many young people who do not understand economics and so they do not believe that the American Dream is within their reach. As a result, they squander their resources and miss golden opportunities to improve their circumstances and that of their families. They seem to have the philosophy of the young Italian-American boy in the book *Knock on Any Door*—they want to live fast, die young, and have a good-looking corpse.

In the process, they miss opportunities to improve their financial position. An excellent example is my firm, DHA. Many of our engineers have been with us since the early days of DHA. At that time, they could have bought a share of DHA stock for between $1 and $5 per share. Today it is worth $645.94 a share. I have been encouraged to split the stock but I have refused. First, if I split the stock I have no evidence that our people will buy it—they did not buy when it was less than $10.00—even though it can be purchased via payroll deduction. Second, the value of stock ownership does not increase with a stock split. You have more shares, but the total value of the shares owned does not change—that is, the price of each share decreases. Some of our employees have joined DHA and left after a few years with thousands of dollars in profit. But others have not participated in the employee stock program at all. A similar situation exists regarding our 401(k) plan. There is very little participation among our lower paid staff in this very beneficial program.

* * *

In my opinion, the key ingredient for success in America is the belief that regardless of the circumstances of birth, or the socioeconomic level of your parents, you can achieve the American Dream if you are willing to fight hard to overcome the roadblocks that might lie ahead.

Two friends from the neighborhood I grew up in vividly validate that doctrine. Both grew up in the Ida B. Wells Homes low-income housing project located across the street from where I lived.

I met Dr. Donald H. Smith while studying at the University of Illinois. When I first met him I assumed, based on the manner in which he spoke and dressed, that he was from an affluent family. Many years later, by reading his biography, I learned he was from a single-parent home headed by his mother. One day, without saying a word to him, she went to California, where she remained for an extended period of time. Don continued with his schooling and worked part-time jobs to provide funds so he could survive and continue his high school education. He went on to receive a doctorate in education from the University of Wisconsin and had an illustrious career in education, eventually becoming a professor at New York University. Subsequently, an endowed invitational lecture series was established in his name at NYU. He received other prominent national awards, too.

I met Reuben Cannon through his wife and my dear friend, Alice Wiggins Tolbert. Reuben also lived in the Ida B. Wells Homes project in Chicago. Reuben was eight years old when his father died and his mother told him he was now "the man of the family." He took those words to heart and began seeking ways to earn money for his family. He began by delivering newspapers, then went on to other jobs as he grew older. He studied the needs of each job that he took and determined what was necessary for him to be successful at it. For example, he recognized that the key to being successful as a paperboy was to get his clients to pay him on schedule. To try to make that happen, he went the "extra mile" to get to know his clients and have them like and respect him. His last job before leaving Chicago was in the steel mills in Indiana. While in that position he was invited by a friend in Los Angeles to come to California to seek his fortune. Ruben moved to Los Angeles and slept on his friend's couch until he landed a permanent job. His goal was to become a movie, radio, television, and Broadway producer.

Each day, Reuben would join other day laborers looking for work in the Los Angeles entertainment industry. Following many unsuccessful weeks seeking work, Reuben was hired as a part-time day laborer to work in a company mail room after two employees at the company went skiing for the weekend and decided not to return. Eventually he was hired as a permanent employee. Delivering the mail to the various departments gave Reuben the opportunity to learn about the entertainment business. One day, he was offered a better-paying job in another department. In response to the offer, Reuben asked the head man if anyone from that department had ever become a producer. The man replied no, so Reuben said the equivalent of "thanks but no thanks" and remained in the mail room. Eventually he was offered a job that could lead to his becoming a producer. He took it, and the rest is history. Reuben today is a very successful producer of stage, screen, and television. On December 8, 2011, Sonia and I had the pleasure of sitting with Reuben and his wife, Alice Wiggins Tolbert, at the opening night of his new production on Broadway, "Stick Fly," which followed his Broadway hit "The Color Purple." I am sure Reuben will have many more hits to come in the years ahead.

Eleven

Engineering Public Policy

I HAVE always loved to travel and to explore new places. True to the engineer that I am, I not surprisingly especially enjoy observing and learning about different approaches to engineering dreams and problems around the world while traveling.

Few places have produced as many engineering feats as China. This is the country, after all, that built the longest wall in the world (the Great Wall), the longest artificial river in the world (the Grand Canal), and the largest earth-filled dam in the world (the Three Gorges Dam). That's in addition to building some of the most complex bridges, buildings, and other structures in the world.

In 2010 Sonia and I took our second trip to China. We wanted to visit Xian, one of the oldest cities in China, see the terra-cotta soldiers, visit Beijing and

Shanghai, ride trains going over 200 miles per hour, and see the Three Gorges Dam. As a geotechnical engineer, that one was a must for me.

Our trip was an awakening.

Ten years earlier, in 2000, Sonia and I had visited China while I was president of the American Society of Civil Engineers, making an official visit to Beijing to meet with the leadership of Chinese Civil Engineering and Construction, the agency responsible for handling the contract for everything from rail construction to hotel management in China. What we saw in Beijing on our visit back then was an old city with limited conveniences, whose principal mode of transportation was the bicycle.

What we saw in 2010 in Beijing, in Shanghai, and in Xian were vibrant major cities where the automobile is king and where modern road, rail, and public transportation systems are now the norm.

When we were in China in 2000, the Third Ring Road around Beijing was nearing completion, but most people still got around by bicycle. Today, there are eight ring roads around Beijing. Automobile traffic is heavy all day, and bicycles are a rarity. Relatively new rail transit lines in Beijing and Shanghai efficiently transport passengers throughout these cities and to the airports, oftentimes by high-speed rail networks that other countries—the United States included—can only dream about. China has the world's biggest network of high-speed rail, with 5,800 miles of rail linking the massive country's biggest cities together.

I love train travel and was thrilled to ride a train traveling in excess of 250 miles per hour while in China. While there, I also attended an international high-speed rail conference in Beijing and was told that there's a high-speed rail line under construction to provide service between Beijing and Shanghai that, I was told, is designed to travel at a speed in excess of 300 miles per hour. I would love to ride it. Unfortunately, I doubt I will live long enough to experience such travel in the United States.

All of the airports we flew into when visiting Beijing, Shanghai, and Xian were modern, efficient, and huge. All but the airport in Xian were served by rail, both high speed and conventional subway. Roadway systems were in good shape. We also were very impressed by the large number of relatively new high-rise buildings and unique structures in China's major cities. Beijing and its buildings were on the world's stage with the 2008 Olympic Games, and structures such as the "Birds Nest" National Stadium and the "Water Cube" swimming center, as well as unique structures such as its Capital International Airport and South Railway

Station, captured the eye and the imagination of engineers, architects, and millions of Olympic spectators.

Sonia was shaken when we got to the hundredth floor of a high-rise building with glass floors which allowed one to look down to the first floor. As a result, we did not remain at the top level long.

Outside of Beijing, Sonia and I took a Yangtze River cruise because I wanted to visit the Three Gorges Dam. I had visited the dam in the year 2000, back when it was still very much under construction. When we visited the dam again ten years later it was nearly complete, and many of its thirty-two massive electricity generating turbines were already in operation. Three Gorges is truly a vast engineering feat, measuring nearly 600 feet high and spanning more than 7,600 feet across. The project required nearly thirty million cubic meters of concrete and 463,000 tons of steel—enough to build more than sixty Eiffel Towers. Prior to the filling of the dam, people living in the region to be covered by water were moved to new homes built by the government above the maximum reservoir level. It is claimed that the replacement homes are larger and better constructed than the ones covered by water and have more amenities.

I think China's progress in its major cities since my first visit there in 2000 was made possible because the country is using its financial resources to build, maintain, and modernize the infrastructure needed to serve its 1.3 billion people instead of using its financial resources to shore up other countries and build its image as a superpower. Another reason for the vast improvement of China's infrastructure since 2000, I think, stems from the fact that the higher echelon of its national government is highly populated by engineers, who realize that infrastructure is extremely important to the health and welfare of its nation and its people.

My most recent trip to China led me to reflect on how we use our resources—both technical and human—in America.

I believe I have lived in the best of times for our country. When I was in my twenties, Dwight D. Eisenhower was president. Our country built the Interstate Highway System that was the envy of the world. We built the most modern airports in the world, including Dulles International Airport in Washington, which Eisenhower himself dedicated in 1962 and my firm much later was fortunate enough to work on. We upgraded the nation's bridges and roads and rail systems.

In a nutshell, we invested in America.

Back then, President Eisenhower also warned us about a potential threat to our country and all the progress we had made. The US Army general turned president warned us of the growing "military-industrial complex" and what it might mean to our economy, our political system, and our future in America. We have not heeded President Eisenhower's warning. Each year, more of our national financial resources are being squandered by excessive defense and foreign aid spending and inadequate spending on infrastructure, education, and the health and welfare of the American people.

In 2010 we spent about $680 billion on the Department of Defense. By comparison, we invested less than $90 billion in our roads, rail, sewer systems, and other types of transportation and water infrastructure in America. Yes, we need a strong national defense, and yes we need to support our allies in other countries. But do we need to spend nearly eight times on defense what we spend on building our own country? While defense spending has increased dramatically year after year after year, spending on infrastructure has declined dramatically.

The wars in Iraq and Afghanistan were wars of choice, not of necessity. They placed a heavy burden on our treasury as well as the health and welfare of our people. Getting rid of Saddam Hussein and trying to rid Afghanistan of the Taliban, although noble in concept, are not worth the economic strain nor human lives our country is paying, especially when one considers that much of the financial and material resources we are putting into other countries are being consumed by graft, corruption, and thievery while the United States looks the other way.

My saddest moments in recent years have been when I took the time to read the stories and see the faces of Americans killed in Iraq, Afghanistan, and Pakistan that were periodically carried in the *Washington Post*. What a waste. But along with wasting so many lives, we have wasted so much money in those countries. According to a Harvard University study, the United States spent about $2 trillion for military campaigns in Afghanistan and Iraq. But that's just a fraction of the monetary costs we'll all bear. The Harvard study estimates that US taxpayers will spend as much as three times that amount—a total of $4 trillion to $6 trillion—when the medical care for wounded veterans, repairs and upgrades to military equipment, and other costs are included. And that doesn't include the billions of dollars we'll spend rebuilding and providing aid to the countries we helped destroy.

At the same time, the infrastructure of our nation rapidly deteriorates, and many of our citizens are in dire need. Just think what we could do for our country if we had only a fraction of the money we've spent in Iraq and Afghanistan to spend here. It makes no sense that we spend that sort of money in other countries, especially when much of our largess is wasted through fraud and theft and our soldiers are being killed by soldiers and police native to the countries we are there to help.

Even without our egregious spending on defense and our financing improvements in other countries, America has not paid sufficient attention to our infrastructure. I have told my engineering friends that over the years we have done our jobs too well. The infrastructure we design and construct generally is kept in service and lasts much longer than its predicted design life. Take bridges as an example. Nearly a third of the 607,000-plus bridges in America have exceeded their design life of fifty years, according to the 2013 American Society of Civil Engineers' Report Card for America's Infrastructure. Some drinking water systems in America still have pipes that date back to before the Civil War. Outdated public sewer pipelines and wastewater treatment facilities help lead to the discharge of 900 billion gallons of untreated sewage into our waterways, our streets, and our homes each year. The 2013 ASCE Report Card survey gives America a pitiful D+ for its infrastructure. To bring our nation's bridges, highways, and water and wastewater facilities up to modern-day standards, ASCE estimates that America needs to invest $3.6 trillion in infrastructure improvements because we've delayed spending and repairs for far too long.

America and its leaders don't think about these things, however, until we have a major failure, like we did with the levees in New Orleans after Hurricane Katrina in 2005 or the collapse of the I-35 bridge in Minneapolis in 2007. Then, instead of properly addressing these problems and millions more waiting to happen nationwide, we seek a scapegoat. Unfortunately it appears that the only thing that can get our leaders' attention is a catastrophe. But what they don't see is that the dire state of our national infrastructure is a catastrophe.

America can't remain in a position to help other nations if we don't first help keep our own country strong, vibrant, and prosperous. And we can't do that with bridges that are crumbling, pipes and sewers that leak, and roads and airports that are inadequate to serve our population. We must begin thinking of America first, and postpone thinking about controlling the rest of the world. History has shown us that every nation that overextended itself throughout the world, while ignoring its own needs and the needs of its people back home, has eventually failed. We should take care of America first if we don't want this to happen.

The engineer and public policy

When I entered the engineering profession it was against the engineers' code of ethics to be actively involved in politics. Unfortunately that limitation prevented engineers from seriously engaging in political activities, and in my opinion that has harmed our profession and our nation. Among the 535 members of the 112th Congress, there were a total of six engineers according to the Congressional Research Service. Therefore, when it comes to matters involving the public infrastructure, it's hard to see how members of Congress have adequate knowledge and experience to properly consider what's best for our country—and ultimately, the public health and safety issues that are tied to basic necessities like water and sewer systems and maintaining the safety and adequacy of our highways and airports.

I strongly believe that the engineering profession needs greater representation among elected officials to both better protect public health safety and welfare and to more wisely spend our infrastructure dollars. Unfortunately this view does not appear to be shared by my engineering brethren. We do nothing but complain while our professional vision of the role of engineers in politics remains nearly the same as it was when I was an undergraduate student in the early 1950s. The result remains damaging to our profession and nation.

I have tried to practice what I preach, but I have not been successful.

During President Clinton's first term, I vied for the position of assistant secretary of the Army for Civil Works. That position oversees the US Army Corps of Engineers, so it's a natural position for an engineer. I nearly made it. I had two interviews with the secretary of defense, among others. I was told I got approved all the way up to Vice President Gore. Unfortunately, I was told, he turned me down. My understanding is that I was not "green enough." If that's the case, I'm not sure how he would have known, since he never interviewed me for the position. Incidentally, I received no support from engineering professional organizations during this quest. Nor did I get any assistance from the Congressional Black Caucus. My only real support came from the Texas delegation in the US House, through the effort of Rep. Eddie Bernice Johnson. I am deeply indebted to her for her leadership on my behalf and the support given to my candidacy by the Texas delegation in the House. I do not believe they knew I was a Texan by birth.

During the administration of President George W. Bush, I had an excellent opportunity to achieve my goal of serving our nation through serving our government. One day, I received a call from my friend the Honorable Norman Mineta, who was then secretary of transportation. When I answered the phone, he opened the conversation with, "Delon, are you ready to come into government?" Unfortunately he caught me by surprise. "It depends on the position," I replied. The response, though truthful, was impolitic I guess. Any suggestions of my coming to work for him or for President Bush ultimately fell by the wayside, and our conversation ended gracefully. Secretary Mineta is now working for a public affairs firm in Washington. We meet periodically for lunch and, in the process, keep each other abreast of our professional careers. It is something of an unspoken subject between us now, but I deeply regret that I blew the opportunity to serve my country under Secretary Mineta.

I am grateful for his friendship.

TWELVE

Reflections on a Life Constructed

I GOT the idea to write this book after reading *The Last Lecture* authored by Randy Pausch. Pausch was a computer science professor at Carnegie Mellon University when he discovered in September 2006 that he had pancreatic cancer and did not have long to live. He and his wife had two very young children, and he wanted to leave something for them to remember him by and to provide guidance for them as they grew toward maturity and beyond. I did not know Pausch (despite the fact that he was raised in Columbia, Maryland, not too far from where I live), but his words and his attitude impressed me, like they have impressed millions of others. His book contains the stories of his childhood, the lessons he hopes his children will learn, and thanks for his family and friends for the successes and accomplishments throughout his life.

Like Pausch, I wanted to write a book that would include some lessons on life, business, and the engineering profession that would be of some value to my family, friends, and others. I hope I've been able to convey some of that.

My life has been rich and fulfilling. But what would I change if I had the opportunity to live it over again?

One thing I would do differently is somewhat esoteric but is in keeping with my values when it comes to education and business. I think I would have added either a law degree or a degree in business administration to my credentials. Doing so would have helped me to accomplish even more, but it also could have made the lives of others better.

The other things I would do differently are more personal.

First, I would have a family with children. In my earlier days I focused more on building a business than I did on building a family. After eighty years of living, I think about what will remain when I am gone. There will be office complexes and airports and railway stations that I helped bring into this world. But there will be no children. I had the opportunity to have children, but I missed it. I hope others don't.

Second, I would be more involved with my family and friends. I've come to realize that they are the most important things in life. Have them foremost in mind when you make every life decision. For me, it wasn't easy, given the unusual circumstances involving my birth mother and family in Texas, the mother who raised me in Chicago, and the rest of my family scattered in between. But I could have done a better job of understanding, being involved in, and supporting the family that I did have.

I'm thankful for the family and the friends that I have had.

Thanks to the support of my mother, Elizabeth, and my friends and co-workers, coupled with my willingness to work hard, play to win, and to assume risks, I was able to meet with some success in life. I would not be where I am today without the strong support I have received from family and friends. I humbly hope that in some small way I have enriched their lives as well.

I've honored my family in the best way an engineer can: by building their legacy into some of the projects I've been involved with. Hopefully, there will be more to come.

Several years ago, two officers in the US Navy's Seabees unit, Admiral Benjamin Montoya and Captain William Hilderbrand, came to visit me in my office in Washington. They told me that a team of retired Seabees had been assembled to lead an effort to raise funds to build and furnish a new Seabee Museum at the Port Hueneme Naval Base in California. As an engineer and a former navy reservist, they asked if I would be interested in being a member of the board of the museum. I readily agreed. At the time of this writing, we have raised the money to renovate the structure to house the museum exhibits, and it is now in use. However, we have not yet raised sufficient funds to complete all the planned exhibit areas. I attended the opening of the renovated museum building. The ceremony was impressive, the crowd was enthusiastic, the museum store sales were brisk, and everyone appeared to be having a wonderful time. A very bright future lies ahead for the Seabee Museum. We shall complete our fundraising activities and complete and install all the planned exhibits in the near future. Come visit. The courtyard at the main entrance to Seabee Museum will be made of engraved bricks to honor the remembrance of loved ones. I plan to have engraved bricks placed there in honor of my mother, Elizabeth, my birth mother, Alzadie, and my brother, Clarence.

I have always dreamed of honoring my birth mother, Alzadie Lewis Douglas, and the mother who raised me, Elizabeth Lewis Hampton. I am halfway there. In September 2012, Purdue University dedicated and named its principal civil engineering building the Delon and Elizabeth Hampton Hall of Civil Engineering. I wish my mother could have been there to enjoy the ceremony. In a way she was, as a picture of me with her was unveiled as a permanent fixture in the building bearing our names. It was a gratifying and humbling occasion, and I am grateful for the friends and family from across the country that traveled to Purdue to attend.

My next goal is to establish a fitting tribute for my birth mother, Alzadie Lewis Douglas. I regret I did not know her. But I do know that she was a woman who was wise beyond her age. Only twenty-five years old when I was born, she made the critical decision while on her deathbed that impacted my future forever. I want to honor her for that decision. Currently, I'm thinking about doing that in a way that recognizes my other occupation in life, as a professor. I think I would like to endow in her name an annual lecture series on civil engineering at a major research university or fund a professorship at same.

The engineering profession has been good to me. It has allowed me to provide well for my family, to travel the world, and to be honored by my peers.

Yes, building the business and the life I have constructed has left some voids in my personal life that can never be filled, and some regrets that I didn't focus more on family, friends, and other areas. But over-all, the life I have constructed has been a wonderful life—one that has given me the opportunity to serve my family, my country, and my profession.

To all who contributed to my success and happiness, thanks a million.

APPENDIX

A Bit of Douglas History

CHARLES DOUGLAS was a slave who lived and died in Marion County, Texas. It is not certain where he was born, though it has been suggested by at least one family member that he was born in West Africa and came to the United States via the British West Indies.

Marion County is located in Northeast Texas. Jefferson is the county seat. Charles Douglas lived in Smithland, Texas, in a community known as "Douglas Bottom."

Verbal history has it that Charles Douglas managed the plantation of his owner. At some point in time, he purchased his freedom with gold coins. No one knows how he obtained the gold coins.

Once he purchased his freedom, Charles Douglas purchased over one thousand acres of land, with gold coins, near Smithland. He sold parcels of the thousand-plus acres to other slaves as they were freed. The thousand-plus acre parcel of land was named Douglas Bottom. Douglas Bottom has a school (Douglas Chapel School), a church (Douglas Chapel Christian Church), and a cemetery (Douglas Chapel Cemetery). Some of the families who settled in the area were the Harmons, Sassers, Crowes, Lewises, and of course, the Douglases. The church and cemetery are still in existence. Approximately 400 acres of the original acreage remain as a part of the R. D. Douglas, MD, and Willie Mae Douglas estates. I sold my share of the land I inherited to a cousin, Valentine Lewis Jr.

According to Marion County deed and probate records, Charles Douglas

- was a "free man of color" (FMC);
- purchased over a thousand acres near Smithland, Texas;
- married Rosanna; and
- after Rosanna's death, married Georgia Ann.

While married to Georgia Ann, Charles Douglas had several children, among them:

- Charles Douglas Jr.
- John Henry Douglas Sr.

Verbal history has it that Charles Douglas Jr. killed a man in Marion County and subsequently fled the county. He settled in a rural community near Houston and changed his name to Henry Washington. He is buried in Douglas Chapel Cemetery.

John Henry Douglas Sr. founded the John Douglas and Sons Shingle Mill in the early 1900s. The business made shingles for roofs from cypress trees. The shingles were sold and distributed throughout Northeast Texas, Arkansas, Louisiana, and Oklahoma. During its period of operation, the shingle mill employed both blacks and whites, which was very atypical of that era. The mill closed in the early 1940s.

John Henry Douglas Sr. had eight children. Their names are as follows:

1. John Henry Jr.
2. Ida
3. Charles III
4. Raymond
5. Anne
6. Herman
7. Wilson
8. Luther

Charles III had two sons:

1. Clarence Everett Douglas, MD
2. Charles Douglas Jr. (Delon Hampton, PhD, PE)

I have no historical information on the Lewis or Hampton sides of my heritage.

INDEX